Jeremy Black is one of the UK's most respected and prolific historians. He is Emeritus Professor of History at the University of Exeter and a renowned expert on the history of war. He is a Senior Fellow at the Foreign Policy Research Institute. His recent books include *Military Strategy: A Global History*, *A History of the Second World War in 100 Maps*, *Tank Warfare* and *The World of James Bond*. He appears regularly on TV and radio.

A Brief History of the British Monarchy

From the Iron Age to King Charles III

Jeremy Black

ROBINSON

For William Dartmouth

ROBINSON

First published in Great Britain in 2023 by Robinson

13 5 7 9 10 8 6 4 2

Copyright © Jeremy Black, 2022
Illustrations by Liane Payne

A CIP catalogue record for this book
is available from the British Library.

ISBN: 978-1-47214-790-5

Typeset in Scala by Hewer Text UK Ltd, Edinburgh
Printed and bound in Great Britain by Clays Ltd, Elcograf S.p.A.

Papers used by Robinson are from well-managed
forests and other responsible sources.

Robinson
An imprint of
Little, Brown Book Group
Carmelite House
50 Victoria Embankment
London EC4Y 0DZ

An Hachette UK Company
www.hachette.co.uk

www.littlebrown.co.uk

Contents

....

Preface

....

Identity is found through place and experience, the two combining in the history of a country. However resented, its government provides part of that identity, and for Britain, as for many other states, monarchy has played a major role in that history. Relatively unusually in international terms today, Britain is still a monarchy like several other European countries and principalities, as well as a range of non-Western states including Saudi Arabia, Thailand and Japan. The history of both Britain and its monarchy in part requires an understanding of why that continuity is the case. At this modern turning point, just after the reign of the longest-living British monarch, it is important to understand the past and present of the monarchy, so that we can assess its relevance for the present and the future. Elizabeth II (1952–2022) was a key figure, one who preserved the lineage of monarchy but also changed it to provide a current context for a present that looks toward the future.

An understanding of British monarchy is a fascinating as well as important story, one that consistently involved the interplay of individuals and institutions. The former became clearer with time; with George III (1760–1820) there are regular and plentiful letters written by the king in his own hand, and this practice became more common. As a result, it is from then that it is easier to consider the individual from, as it were, the inside. Nevertheless, all the monarchs have been of consequence, and the history of British monarchy begins far back in time.

It is a great pleasure to thank Emma Smith for asking me to write this book. I have benefited from many decades teaching British history and from having already written biographies of

> ## The March of Time
>
> 'The prince's most secret counsels, motives and pursuits, will probably one day be published and rigorously judged; and, however flattered whilst living, yet when dead, he will be treated as his actions have deserved, with honour or reproach, with veneration or contempt.'
>
> Nicholas Tindal, translation of Paul de Rapin-Thoyras' *History of England* (1725–3), dedicated to Frederick, Prince of Wales

two kings and of one dynasty. I am very grateful indeed to Grayson Ditchfield, Bill Gibson, Will Hay, George Robb, Nigel Saul and Neil York for commenting on an earlier draft of this book. This means an enormous amount given how busy we all are. They are not responsible for any errors that remain. I owe particular points to Daniel Hannan.

It is a great pleasure to dedicate this book to William Dartmouth, a generous friend with a strong and profound interest in history.

Note

Years after a monarch's name are regnal years.

1
Origins

....

The origin of monarchy is complex and we cannot pinpoint a specific date. Instead, we must look back into multiple reigns in a context very different to that of ruling a country. Let us indeed put aside the effort by James Howell, Historiographer Royal, who, in *A Discourse Concerning the Precedency of Kings* (1664), managed to present Britain as a 'Royal Isle' even prior to the Roman period. In practice, monarchy began in Britain as tribal leadership.

This leadership was a widespread practice that drew on the need for a single leader in conflict and in matters within the tribe, notably the maintenance of order and the administration of justice. Records are very limited for the character of this leadership, other than from the first century BCE, but Roman sources provide material on those rulers with which they came into contact. This was the case not so much with Julius Caesar's limited expeditions in 55 and 54 BCE which encountered tribal opposition, but rather of the process of conquest that began in 43 CE. Some of those were opponents, notably Caratacus, the leader of the Catuvellauni, and Boudica, Queen of the Iceni, both of whom were finally overcome, while several became allies, particularly Cogidubnus, ruler of the Atrebates, and Cartimandua, Queen of the Brigantes.

Separately, a different form of monarchy was imposed on what became Roman Britain, that of a distant emperor. Indeed, in 43 CE, the year of the next invasion, the Emperor Claudius arrived in a Britain that existed only in the topographical sense, not socially or politically, thus associating himself with a hitherto successful conquest. Other emperors who came to Britain included Hadrian in 122 CE, driving forward the construction of a wall from the North to the Irish Sea, Septimius Severus in

Female Rule

Cartimandua, Queen of the Brigantes (c. 43–69), was a figure of lesser fascination to later commentators than Boudica, but provided an opportunity to discuss rule by women. In his *The History of the County of Cumberland* (1794), William Hutchinson was clearcut:

> 'In those days, it was no disgrace, to the bravest people, to be governed by a woman; disgustful effeminancies had not then contaminated the sex . . . Even men inured to indefatigable labours and toils, constantly in arms, subsisting chiefly by warfare or the chase, and bred up to feats of valour and the simple rules of native honour, were not ashamed to be led to battle by a woman . . . nor is the history of Cartimandua blotted, till, by the intercourse of the Romans, the native virtue of the Brigantes was corrupted.'

In an idealised morality tale, Hutchinson presented luxury and wealth as bringing corruption and vice, with the queen expelling her husband and taking his armour-bearer to her bed.

208–211 CE, invading Caledonia (modern Scotland), only to die of disease at Eboracum (York), Constantius Chlorus in 296, and Constantine in 306.

Foreign rule was the first force that linked what was to become England (bar Northumbria) and Wales in one state; and this began a pattern in which Britain had a variety of monarchical systems. Roman accounts also provide what we know of ancient Britain, beyond what archaeology can reveal.

Invading Caledonia (Scotland)

'. . . as he advanced through the country he experienced countless hardships in cutting down the forests, levelling the heights, filling up the swamps and bridging the rivers . . . Severus did not desist until he approached the extremity of the island. Here he observed most accurately the variation of the sun's motion and the length of the days and the nights in summer and winter respectively . . . conveyed in a covered litter most of the way on account of his infirmity.'

Cassius Dio of Septimius Severus, 208–211

Roman imperial monarchy was provided not just for soldiers and settlers, but also for non-Roman subjects. This monarchy was more potent due to its role in religion, notably the cults of the Olympian gods which the Romans introduced. Subsequently, the possible long-term implications of Christianity becoming the state religion in the fourth century are unclear, for Roman Britain was weakened by a crucial failing of the imperial monarchy. This was the inability to devise a consistently accepted system of imperial succession, and the related willingness of military units to support their commanders in bids for power. This process directly affected Britain.

This was notably so in 406 when Gaul (France) was invaded by 'barbarians', and Britain, threatened with being cut off from the rest of the Empire, ended up with its own self-styled 'Roman Emperor', Constantine III, his name and number a claim to prestige, legitimacy and longevity. This *de facto* autonomy, however, did not lead to independence. Constantine took most of Britain's military forces to Gaul, but these troops did not return and he was killed in 411. Meanwhile, the disillusioned Romano-Britons had expelled his administrators and appealed to the true Emperor, Honorius, for the restoration of legitimate rule and for help accordingly. Hard-pressed in Italy by the Goths, who, under Alaric, were to storm Rome itself in 410, he could only tell them to look to their own defences.

Roman Dynastic 'Magic'

Magnus Maximus, who claimed the Roman Empire in 383, was commander in Britain from 380 and took much of the garrison with him to Gaul in 383. Recognised as Emperor in much of the West in 384, he was defeated in Italy in 388 and executed. Magnus was presented in the medieval Welsh legend *Breuddwynd Macsen Wledig* as Macsen Wledig, founder of a number of major lineages. This unfounded claim was designed to support the pretensions of the dynasty of Gwynedd. The long shadow cast by Rome was seen in it providing the fount of legitimate political authority. Welsh rulers also established their courts on Roman sites.

The post- (or sub-) Roman British divided into warring kingdoms (albeit in a process for which information is limited) based on locally powerful warlords, such as Maelgwyn (d. 547), ruler of Gwynedd, or north-west Wales. The most famous of these warlords, Arthur, is a legendary figure, whose historicity is a matter of both controversy and contention. So also with Vortigern, a fifth-century figure later referred to as a king of the Britons or as a usurper. In terms of the numbers of kings in British history, the centuries from 400 to 700 contributed the largest number. These kingdoms mounted a long resistance to invasion by the Angles and Saxons, and were celebrated in poetry, the survival of which is seen as starting with Aneirin and Taliesin in the sixth century. Aneirin's poem described his lord, Mynyddog Mwyn-fawr of Edinburgh, while Taliesin wrote in praise of Unrien of Rheged, a principality around the Solway, and his son Owain. After much conflict, the kingdoms of Elmet, centred on Leeds, and Rheged were absorbed by the Anglian kingdom of Northumbria in the late sixth and seventh centuries. Conquest, however, remained incomplete, the kingdoms in Wales continuing independent, while, as an indication of violence, the use of hillforts revived.

The ethic of the warband was important to the invaders, and remained so thanks to the length of the conquest period. These warbands were led by warriors who were probably tribal figures, although some of the early names that have survived may well be of mythical figures, such as the Jutish brothers Hengist and Horsa, the former of whom allegedly conquered Kent. Conquest tipped the balance between the Anglo-Saxon kingdoms. Those distant from the frontier of advance, such as Kent, East Anglia, and Lindsey (in Lincolnshire), lost out in power, and eventually independence, to kingdoms further west, to the Saxon kingdom of Wessex (in the West Country) and its Anglian counterparts of Mercia (in the Midlands), Deira (Yorkshire), and Bernicia (the North-East). Their expansion interacted with the coalescence of the numerous small Anglo-Saxon kingdoms. With time, and especially after 700, ruling houses were increasingly differenti-ated from landowners, and royal justice from that of kin, feud and surety. At the apex was what was to be called a *Bretwalda*: wide ruler or over-king.

Initially, Kent took a major part. Aethelbert, King of Kent (*c.*583–616) played a key role in the conversion of Britain to Catholicism, as he welcomed St Augustine who was sent from Rome by Pope Gregory the Great in 597. The king's wife, Bertha, a Frankish princess, had already been allowed to practise her Christianity. The rapidly converted king supported Augustine in establishing three bishoprics: at Canterbury, London and Rochester. As a result of the influence of Kent, Canterbury, its capital, not London, was the see of the Archbishop. Christian kingship meant a need to incorporate a role for the clergy. It also ensured that polygamy would not be acceptable and thus helped clarify the position of queens as opposed to new sexual favourites of the king. The role of queens was to owe a lot to their linkage with ecclesiastical foundations.

The kings of Northumbria, the kingdom created from Bernicia and Deira, and thus stretching from the Firth of Forth to the Humber producing a far-flung state, were similarly central to conversion by the Irish Church via its Scottish base at Iona. King Oswy (642–70) played a major role in ensuring that at the Synod (church meeting) of Whitby in 664, Roman, rather than Celtic, customs prevailed. Rulers also took an important part in founding monasteries, Oswald of Northumbria helping establish Lindisfarne in 635. For much of the seventh century, Northumbria provided the *Bretwalda*. It also had the Venerable Bede (*c.*673– 735), a monk whose *Ecclesiastical History of the English People* (*c.*731), dedicated to king Ceolwulf (729–37), provided the idea of an Anglo-Saxon foundation of nationhood, with a *witan* (council) and elected kings, which was to offer later generations, especially in the seventeenth, eighteenth and nineteenth centuries, the notion of an ancient constitution with the king as bound by law as well as law-giver.

Defeat in 678, however, had led to the end of Northumbrian hegemony, with its replacement in that role, Mercia, having already absorbed or dominated other kingdoms, notably those of the Hwicce and the Magonsaetan and, from 654, East Anglia. The struggle between Mercia and Northumbria, more generally, dominated the period 630–800, being won by Mercia.

The British kingdoms were now largely just adjuncts. As with the Anglo-Saxons, there was a process of consolidation, with a decline in the number of kingdoms, as the less successful, such as Gower, Gwent, Ergyng, Ceredigion, Builth, Brycheiniog and Powys, all in Wales, were taken over. The most expansive in Wales were Gwynedd in the north-west, Deheubarth in the south-west and Glywysing in the south-east, the kingdoms based on the largest amount of fertile lowland, but also benefiting from a degree of immunity from the English. In contrast, Powys in the north-east suffered considerably at the hands of Mercia, while English pressure may also have been responsible in part for the demise of the kingdoms in the Upper Wye. Powys lost Cheshire, Shropshire and Herefordshire to English expansion; a principality that might have served as the base for a strong state being fatally weakened.

Offa (757–96) increased Mercian power, controlling such formerly independent kingdoms as Essex, Kent and Sussex, while Wessex recognised Mercian protection in 786. Offa had aspirations to be in effect king in England. After the defeat of Northumbria, he used the term 'king of the English' at least once in his charters. Offa also sought to have the Mercian church, with its see of Lichfield, given archepiscopal equality with Canterbury and York. Offa's effective control of the commercial centre of London was an important source of liquidity, and also significant to the emergence of the city. Offa is most famous today, however, for the ditched rampart known as Offa's Dyke, running from the Severn estuary to the River Dee. The Dyke was probably a defensive work as well as a boundary.

Offa's success, nevertheless, could not provide lasting unity, largely because of the limited ability of his successors and due to the uncertainty of Mercian control over subsidiary kingdoms. His immediate successor, Coenwulf (796–821), harshly suppressed a rebellion in Kent in 798, issued several charters from London, and suspended Archbishop Wulfred of Canterbury. In the 820s, however, Wessex came to the fore, not least through conquering South-East England. Beornwulf of Mercia (823–6), who deposed Ceolwulf (821–3), was heavily defeated by Egbert of Wessex (802–39) at Ellandum near Swindon in 825 and, in 826, he was defeated by the rebellious East Anglians, while Wessex forces successfully invaded Kent. Not only Mercia but also Northumbria acknowledged the overlordship of Egbert, but effective control over England was beyond Wessex's capability, and Mercia was able to regain the independence lost in 829. Wessex, however, delivered success against the Vikings on a number of occasions across the ninth century. Egbert defeated a joint Viking-Cornish force in 834 and Aethelwulf defeated the Vikings in 851. The frequency of conflict in the history of the period underlined the role of the kings as warriors. At the same time, their functions included internal arbiter, notably as lawgiver and as protector of the church.

A divided England proved vulnerable to Viking invasion, and, in 871, with East Anglia and Yorkshire already conquered, Wessex had to agree to pay tribute to the Vikings, Mercia following in 874. Subordinate kings, alongside territory settled by the conquerors, appeared to be the fate of England, with its monarchical destiny an interplay of local Viking overlord-kings, Scandinavian monarchs, and residual rulers, both Romano-British in Wales and Cumbria, and Anglo-Saxon tributary kings in Wessex and west Mercia: in 877, east and north Mercia had been annexed by the Vikings.

This prospect was brought down by defeat. Alfred of Wessex (871–99) was to be a national hero in later English history, and his successes against the Vikings from 872 were crucial to the curtailing of Viking attack. At the same time, England was divided, with the lands east and north of Watling Street, the Danelaw, left to the Vikings.

The role of contingency in the creation and development of kingdoms was shown by the different fate of Gwynedd under Rhodri Mawr (d. 878), who claimed descent from Magnus Maximus and the sixth-century ruler of Gwynedd, Maelgwyn. He also ruled Powys, which he inherited from his uncle in 855, and Seisyllwg in central Wales which he took over in 871 when his brother-in-law, the ruler, died. Rhodri, however, was pressed hard by the Vikings, and was finally defeated in Anglesey in 867 by invading Mercians.

Alfred was not only victorious but also developed the image and reality of civic kingship (as opposed to just military kingship), setting a pattern for what was to become the Old English Monarchy. Aside from his important military measures and minting good (sound) pennies, a clear sign of a well-established kingdom, Alfred produced a law-code, patronised learning, and established schools. Seeking to sustain his image, he commissioned a biography, *The Life of King Alfred* (893), from Bishop Asser. This stressed his suffering and endurance, presenting effective royal leadership in a markedly Christian light. Such an approach was eased because Alfred's power and prestige were increased by the earlier destruction by the Vikings of the other Anglo-Saxon ruling houses.

Alfred also became important to subsequent images of English nationhood. Paintings such as Daniel Maclise's *Alfred the Great in the Camp of the Danes* (1852) reflected the demand for an exemplary national history. In 1778, the carving of a white horse in a hillside near Westbury that was believed to commemorate Alfred's victory over the Danes at Ethandune in 878 was restored, subsequently being repaired on a number of occasions, including 2007.

Alfred's successors helped define an English state with an English monarch. Military success was crucial to both. His eldest son, Edward (later the Elder, 899–924), conquered the Danelaw, first defeating a rival claimant for Wessex, his cousin Aethelwold. Edward and his sister, Aethelflaed, then conquered East Anglia and the East Midlands, reversing earlier Viking gains.

Edward appears to have intended that his dominions be divided between Athelstan, his son by his first wife, who was born in about 894, and his younger half-brother, Aelfweard, but the latter died soon after Edward. In turn, Athelstan was to be succeeded by Edmund (939–46) and Eadred (946–55), the sons of Edward the Elder by his third wife, and then by the sons of the former, Eadwig (955–9) and Edgar (959–75). England was divided between Eadwig and Edgar in 957, but Eadwig died of unknown causes in 959. There was division and uncertainty over Athelstan's achievement and succession, but Edgar would reprise his achievement.

After his conquest of Northumbria in 927, and subsequent victories in 934 and 939, Athelstan (924–39) started to call himself *rex Anglorum* (king of the English) and on his coins became the first Anglo-Saxon king to be shown wearing a crown. He did not marry which was unusual, but may have reflected a vocation for chastity. A warrior-king who was particularly pious, Athelstan was keen on collecting books as well as the relics of saints. Eadred was also described as king of the English, while, in 973, Edgar was the first to be crowned as king of the English. The coronation was important to the formation of a unified English nation, while, in what was to be a totemic image of authority and power, Edgar was rowed in a boat by subordinate British rulers at Chester in 973.

Possibly as a consequence of the influence of Carolingian (the Frankish dynasty of Charlemagne) ideology, specifically the idea of a Christian empire, expressed by Jonas of Orléans and Hincmar of Reims, which influenced Athelstan and Edgar, tenth-century Wessex moved towards a notion of kingship different from that of the amalgam of kingdoms epitomised by Offa. The new English state did not require, nor was constrained by, precise ethnic, tribal or geographical boundaries. This was a far-flung kingship that covered essentially the area of modern England, and, by the standards of the age, an effective state with royal justice combined with a system of law-courts as well as a form of national taxation. At the same time, the intensive lordship shown by the Crown in Wessex and south Mercia was not matched further north, notably in Northumbria.

England was not the only kingdom in the British Isles. The contrast with Wales is instructive for both. Welsh inheritance

Considering the Sources

The critical assessment of sources relating to monarchs is far from new. Thus, the 1815 edition of the *Encyclopedia Britannica* praised Edgar's ability to keep the peace and block invasions, adding:

'The greatness of King Edgar, which is very much celebrated by the English historians, was owing to the harmony which reigned between him and his subjects; and the reason of this good agreement was that the king sided with Dunstan [Archbishop of Canterbury, 959–88] and the [Benedictine] monks, who had acquired a great ascendant over the people. He enabled them to accomplish their favourite scheme of dispossessing the secular canons of all the monasteries; and he consulted them not only in ecclesiastical but also in civil affairs. On these accounts, he is celebrated by the monkish writers with the highest praises; though it is plain, from some of his actions, that he was a man who could be bound neither by the ties of religion nor humanity.'

customs – the division of property among sons – may have made it more difficult to translate territorial gains into more cohesive statehood. Successful leaders might accumulate several kingships and, on their deaths, individual ones would be inherited by particular sons. Thus, Rhodri Mawr's son, Anarawad, succeeded to Gwynedd, and another son, Cadell, to Seisyllwg. Hwyel Dda, Howel the Good (d. 950), a son of Cadell, initially succeeded only to Ceredigion, but through marriage and conquest came to rule most of Wales, becoming the first Welsh king who certainly issued his own coinage. Although the surviving documents date from far later, his prestige was shown by his being proclaimed in the twelfth century as the codifier of Welsh law.

However, Hwyel's death was followed by the collapse of his realm and internecine conflict. Whereas, in England, unity was created by the destruction or weakening of all bar Wessex by the Vikings, in Wales there was no similar consolidation until the Anglo-Normans conquered much of Wales.

During the Roman period and subsequently, the lands north of the Firth of Forth were occupied by Picts whose kings displayed their prowess in warfare and hunting. They also kept sacral figures – wizards or shamans – who underlined the status of the kings within the community. Western Scotland came to be dominated by a Scottish kingdom of Dal Riata, with its major seat of power at Dunadd, which benefited from its association with Christianity. This kingdom absorbed its Pictish counterpart and in about 843, under Kenneth MacAlpin (d. 858), created the new kingdom of Alba (a Gaelic word for Britain) in the ninth century.

The English kingdom came to intervene more in Scotland and, far more, Wales, but each retained independence. Moreover, the kingdom of the Scots developed, overrunning Strathclyde, Lothian and Cumbria in the tenth century. Indeed, what eventually became Scotland included Scots, Picts, Angles and Britons and, until the mid-twelfth century, it was unclear whether Cumbria and Northumbria would be part of England or of Scotland. That the kings of Scotland were to owe fealty and homage to the kings of England for lands they held in northern England subsequently complicated the situation. Scotland did not abandon the northern counties until the Quitclaim, or Treaty, of York in 1237.

While the territorial bounds of English kingship remained unclear, the identity of the ruler became a matter for contention. The continuity of able adult leadership was broken with Edgar's death in 975, as both his sons were young. The unpopular elder one, Edward, was murdered in 978 and the younger, Aethelred 'the Unready' (978–1016), had a relatively long reign, but one that was wrecked by the revival of Viking invasion combined by his own inability to command trust. Paying off invaders through Danegeld did not bring peace. Aethelred was ultimately succeeded by Cnut (1016–35), the younger son of King Sweyn Forkbeard of Denmark, who was to create a North Sea empire. Aethelred had died in 1016, and Cnut then partitioned England with Aethelred's warrior son, Edmund Ironside, Edmund receiving Wessex and Cnut, Mercia. Edmund, however, swiftly died and Cnut then gained the whole kingdom.

Danish conquest was seen as a form of divine judgment. The House of Wessex appeared finished, while the Old English monarchy was now part of an empire. The nature of monarchy was linked to that of the state. Whereas earlier invaders, culminating in the Vikings in the ninth century, had conquered kingdoms, both Cnut in 1016 and William of Normandy in 1066 each seized a kingdom of England.

Danish kings of England showed that kingship and nationality did not always coincide, which anticipated the later situation. Yet, Cnut's approach to his territories as a whole was like that of Offa within England. Far from trying to create one unified kingdom, he, instead, ruled as the king of a number of kingdoms: England, Denmark and Norway. With Cnut murdering those he distrusted, an Anglo-Scandinavian aristocracy was created in England, although Cnut continued the practices of the Old English monarchy. In 1031, Cnut advanced to the River Tay, receiving the submission of Malcolm II of Scotland, which reaffirmed the claims of the Crown of England to overlordship while also securing Malcolm's support against Norway. Godwine, an Englishman trusted by Cnut, was married to Cnut's sister-in-law, Gytha, in 1019, made an earl in 1020 and became, in practice, Cnut's deputy in England as Cnut spent most of the 1020s pursuing his interests in Scandinavia. The report that he commanded the waves to hold back when the tide came in dated from the following century, but Cnut was certainly brutal. He was also polygamous, adding in 1017 Emma, Aethelred's widow, as his official partner, to his English wife Aelfgifu.

Cnut's achievement was challenged by the weaknesses of his sons, Harold Harefoot (a later nickname) and Harthacnut, the surviving sons of Aelfgifu and Emma respectively. Harold was present in England when Cnut died, while Harthacnut stayed in his Danish dominion, which weakened his position. England was in effect divided in 1035–7. In 1037, Alfred and Edward (later the Confessor), the sons of Aethelred and Emma, both in exile in Normandy during Cnut's reign, separately tried to regain control of England. Betrayed by Godwine, Alfred was blinded on the orders of Harold and then died, while an unsuccessful Edward returned to Normandy. Harold controlled all of England from 1037 until his death in 1040, aged twenty-five. Harthacnut then seized power but became unpopular, in part due to heavy taxation. In 1041, he invited his half-brother Edward back to share in ruling, but, still in his early twenties, the unmarried Harthacnut died, possibly poisoned, in 1042. As so often in the history of the British monarchy, the possible consequences were cut short by the brevity of the reign. This was notably so in terms of the willingness to agree to partition, in 957, 1016 and 1035, as well as the growing power of a number of semi-autonomous earls.

In the event, while Magnus I, king of Norway from 1035, became king of Denmark, the house of Wessex was somewhat unexpectedly revived in the person of Aethelred's surviving son, Edward 'the Confessor' (1042–66). He returned with French, more particularly Norman, advisers, including Robert Champart whom he made Bishop of London and then Archbishop of Canterbury. Edward's piety and focus on faith established an important link between the throne and the Church. He subsequently became a saint, being canonised in 1161, and was thought to originate the 'royal touch' for scrofula. He also built Westminster

Abbey, which became the key for the ecclesiological setting of English (later British) monarchy, to the present day, and of the placing of what became the routines, liturgy and ceremony of coronation.

This reign was in hindsight to be overshadowed by the problem of the succession, but the more immediate issue was that of powerful earldoms, and notably so in the person of Godwine, an English protégé of Cnut who had given him the Earldom of Wessex. Married to a Danish princess, Godwine had six sons in contrast to the lack of children from Edward, his son-in-law. Edward sought to lessen Godwin's control, not least by showing favour to the Normans, Viking descendants. An unsuccessful and then successful rebel, Godwine was dominant at the time of his death in 1053, indeed a form of pseudo-monarch albeit without the legitimacy and prestige of dynastic origin and ecclesiastical sanction. Meanwhile, Edward's changing views on the succession and his lack of leadership helped exacerbate political instability.

Godwine's death left his eldest son, Harold, Earl of Wessex, and, after the king, the largest individual landowner in the county. Harold also acted as pseudo-monarch in the important form of military leader, acquiring considerable prestige from successful campaigning in North Wales against Gruffydd ap Llywelyn, who united Wales – in part by slaying rivals. A threat to Harold due to his alignment with Mercia, Gruffydd was deserted by the lesser rulers before being killed by some of his men, his head being delivered to Harold, who also took his wife. This was kingship in the raw, and indeed the latter practice was frequent. Gruffydd's half-brothers were allowed to inherit Gwynedd on condition that they swore allegiance.

Kingship involved submission by others. Earl Leofric of Mercia died in 1057 and his son Aelfgar in 1062, thus easing the path for Harold. Instead, with Aelfgar's sons, Edwin and Morcar, both minors, Harold's major rival was within the house of Godwine, in the person of his volatile and highly competitive younger brother Tostig, Earl of Northumberland. The young Edgar Aetheling, the grandson of Edward's half-brother Edmund Ironside, was far less consequential.

1066 was to be the year of would-be kings, with no fewer than three, as well as two other bidders. Dying on 5 January, Edward the Confessor was scarcely the first monarch to leave a contested succession. Edward's designation of Harold as successor was that by a sick man for which witnesses were few and self-interested. Indeed, the rules of succession were only really tightened by regulation and the affirmation of battlefield success, both in the eighteenth century. The Witan, the great council of the realm, recognised Harold as king, only for his claim to be challenged by Duke William of Normandy, who argued that Edward had promised him the throne in 1051 and that Harold had acknowledged this claim. What would have been a straightforward contest was complicated by a Scandinavian intervention in the shape of Harald Hardrada, King of Norway. The fate of battle saw him defeated by Harold of England at Stamford Bridge, only for the latter to be killed in the English defeat at Hastings.

The Anglo-Saxon claimant to the throne was now Edgar Atheling. Being young and a mere totem figure might not have made much of a difficulty, were it not that the Anglo-Saxon élite had been weakened greatly by Hastings. On Christmas Day, William was acclaimed King in Westminster Abbey. The unification of England by the house of Wessex had ensured that it fell rapidly. The fate of country, state and monarchy, however, was uncertain.

2
Medievial Monarchies

....

The period from the eleventh to the end of the sixteenth century is a sprawling one with apparent continuities alongside major contrasts in fortune between individual monarchs.

THE NORMANS

A ducal dynasty of Viking descent in Normandy, the Normans were subjects of the Crown of France but also autonomous figures in the power-politics of northern France. England gave them a new setting for their dynamic expansionism, and they had a more lasting impact than Cnut, the earlier eleventh-century conqueror.

WILLIAM I

A warrior ruler, William I (1066–87) won and held England as he held Normandy, by success in warfare. That was his claim to fame and the basis of his control. Yet, as king, William proclaimed himself the rightful successor to Edward the Confessor, which was a basis for legitimation, and, in that role, like Cnut, may not at first have intended sweeping changes. Indeed, he left the surviving English earls in power until the extent of resistance resulted in a harsher attitude, including the dispossession of many English landowners. William was a military presence in Britain, notably in England when he suppressed risings in 1067–9, 1075 and 1080, but also when advancing against Malcolm III of Scotland in 1072, forcing him to do homage for Lothian, although Scotland as a whole remained independent.

William also had to face the threat of Scandinavian invasion, against which he assembled a large army in 1085–6. The problems involved in maintaining it may well have prompted the making of *Domesday Book*, an account of English landholding, in order to ascertain his overall resources and those of others. The survey revealed that the Conqueror had a fifth of England's land. Alongside his rights as heir to the English crown, William also exercised rights over feudal vassals. These included the receipt of military service as well as rights of wardship, marriage and escheat over the vassals.

Furthermore, the territorial interests of the Duchy of Normandy, and its serious disputes with expansionist neighbours, the kingdom of France and the County of Anjou, began a continual commitment to Continental power politics by English kings that was to last for centuries, with territories always held there until the fall of Calais in 1558. That, however, might appear a comment in need of reassessment. In practice, there had been an Anglo-Continental monarchy in 1016–42, but that did not have the long consequences of the Norman Conquest.

As part of a major change in the physical setting of the monarch, William himself died as a result of injuries sustained when thrown by his horse in the French town of Mantes which he had burnt as a result of a border conflict. Henry I, Henry II, Richard I, and Henry V were also to die in France. The funeral at Caen was a reminder of the indignity of death. The fat William's body burst open, and the church was filled with a rank odour, according to Orderic Vitalis.

A sense of precariousness, or at least uncertainty, was shown by William's arrangements for his successors. He had four sons and five daughters by his marriage to Matilda of Flanders, but his son Richard predeceased him. As yet, and as part of a more general lack of fixity in royal arrangements, one already repeatedly seen in the tenth and eleventh centuries, there was no clear preference for male primogeniture (succession by the eldest male child) over partible inheritance (division among heirs). William left Normandy to his rebellious eldest son, Robert, about whom reliable information is scanty other than the hostile account by the historian Orderic Vitalis (1075–1142), and England to his second, William II (1087–1100). This allotment of inheritance (Normandy) to the eldest son, and acquisition (England) to the next, was entirely in keeping with contemporary practice. However, such division was unwelcome not only in the ruling family, where there was strong sibling rivalry, but also, due to the circumstances of conquest, to nobles with estates on both sides of the Channel.

WILLIAM II

Robert wished to reunite the inheritance, but a rebellion in his favour in 1088 by many prominent Norman nobles in England, notably Odo of Bayeux, Earl of Kent, half-brother to William I, failed totally due to the vigour of William's response, a vigour in which he was supported by the English troops. The splendour of Bayeux Cathedral is in part a product of the resources taken from England. William then took his cause to Normandy, winning support from some of the nobles there. Robert pawned Normandy to William in 1096, in order to raise funds to go on the First Crusade which took Jerusalem in 1099.

William II was known, from his red face or hair, as Rufus, although, according to Orderic Vitalis, his hair was yellowish. A vigorous ruler, he had a high reputation in knightly circles. In 1092, Rufus occupied Cumbria, while he was also successful against Norman rebels and the French, although less so in Wales. In 1095, Rufus had Earl Robert of Northumbria dispossessed. But William's refusal to support ecclesiastical reform or papal authority led to a serious dispute with the Church that affected his reputation because writers were clerics, notably Eadmer.

Rufus's building of Westminster Hall was important to the settling down of the monarchy at Westminster. This entailed the creation of a set of buildings there that satisfied the residential, administrative and religious needs of the monarchy.

His death in the New Forest was a matter of controversy, and led to accusations of murder, not least on behalf of his younger brother, Henry. The death, however, was probably the result of a hunting accident. His older brother Richard had been more clearly killed in about 1070 as a result of a hunting accident in the New Forest: he collided with an overhanging branch.

Accounts of William II: Contradictions to the Fore

'Never was there a king held in such affection or in such honour by his men.'

Geffrei Gaimar, *History of the English*

'[H]ated by almost all his people and abhorrent to God, exactly as his end proved, because he died his injustice unabated and without him repenting or making any amends.'

Anglo-Saxon Chronicle

'He never married, but was insatiably addicted to obscene fornication and frequent adulteries, giving his subjects a damnable example of shameful debauchery.'

Orderic Vitalis

'He was squarely built, with a ruddy complexion, light blond hair swept back so as to leave his forehead clear . . . sparkling eyes . . . physically strong despite his modest height . . . He would stare at people with a menacing look in his eyes, and intimidate those he was speaking to by adopting a harsh tone and a studied severity. In private and in the chamber with his friends he was easy-going, and relied a great deal on joking. He was in particular a most eloquent critic of his own mistakes, ensuring thereby that any resentment at what he had done dissolved into laughter.'

William of Malmesbury, *The History of the English Kings*

Henry I

The unmarried William was succeeded by Henry (1100–35), who in the immediate crisis rushed to seize the treasury at Winchester and to assert control. This succession led anew to fraternal division over the kingdom, Robert invading England in 1101. Although Henry persuaded him to renounce his claim to be Robert I, relations between the two continued to be difficult, and helped destabilise Robert's position in Normandy. Henry invaded Normandy in 1105 and, the following year, defeated Robert at Tinchebrai, conquering the duchy. Robert was imprisoned until his death in 1134, although his son, William Clito, unsuccessfully maintained his claim.

While subsequently devoting much of his attention to trying to protect his position in Normandy, Henry also sought to develop royal power in England. Notably he did so by expanding royal judicial activity and by the appointment of local and itinerant justices, which was part of his raising of lesser men to high office.

The Dangers of a King

'A king is like a fire – if you are too close, you burn; if you are too far away, you freeze.'

> Petrus Alfonsi, doctor to Henry I who, indeed, could be arbitrary and capricious. Anxiety and opportunity were consistent aspects of court life.

Henry also proved a determined strengthener of royal power in Wales, seeking to overawe both the Welsh rulers and the Anglo-Norman Marcher lords. For example, as far as the latter were concerned, he developed Carmarthen as a royal lordship with a castle and a royal borough, and took control of Pembroke. In addition, Henry invaded North Wales in person in 1114 and 1121.

This was part of the process of mastery that brought somewhat empty promises of submission by the native rulers which, however, made it difficult for them to legitimate any independent position.

Stability in England was to be threatened yet again by the succession. Henry's first wife, Matilda of Scotland, who he married in 1100, was daughter of King Malcolm of Scotland and his Anglo-Saxon wife of the royal line, a saintly wife similar to her mother, St Margaret of Scotland. Henry had two legitimate children, a son and a daughter by Matilda, but none by his second wife, Adeliza of Louvain. Although Henry had over twenty bastards, his sole legitimate son, William, died in the Channel in the wreck of the *White Ship* in 1120, along with everyone on the vessel bar a butcher. It ran aground on a rock off Barfleur. Henry therefore turned to his widowed daughter Matilda. Twenty-five years old in 1128, she married the fourteen-year-old Geoffrey Plantagenet, heir to the Duke of Anjou, the territory to the south of Normandy. This marriage was largely pursued so that Henry could strengthen his position in Normandy. They had a son, the future Henry II, in 1133, thus establishing the dynasty.

STEPHEN

When, however, Henry died in 1135, the throne was seized by his nephew Stephen (1135–54), son of William I's daughter Adela by Stephen, Count of Blois, who had been killed on the First Crusade. Blois bordered Normandy. As Count of Mortain, Stephen had an independent position in France. Harmed by falling out with the powerful, including Roger, Bishop of Salisbury, the Treasurer, in 1139, his reign in England was nearly as disastrous as that of Aethelred the Unready. Stephen was unable to maintain control in England (or Normandy) and in 1139 Matilda invaded. In the subsequent conflict, Matilda captured Stephen at the battle of Lincoln in 1141, but, as a reminder of the differences of events, this was no Tinchebrai. Matilda was unable to consolidate her position, in part due to the energetic opposition of another Matilda, Stephen's wife, and soon after exchanged Stephen for her captured half-brother, Robert, Earl of Gloucester, the most talented of Henry's illegitimate children. Although Stephen was successful against Matilda in England, Geoffrey completed the conquest of Normandy. In 1152, in turn, his heir, Henry, invaded England.

This civil war was the most serious and sustained of the internal dynastic conflicts between 1066 and the Wars of the Roses, but far from the only one. These conflicts were in part normative, a product of the élite bellicosity that helped make peaceful settlements to disputes difficult, and this situation was accentuated by the problems posed by a trans-Channel inheritance. The last was the key issue in the contested succession to William I. There was to be no inheritance by illegitimate children.

The nobility on both sides wanted peace, and to keep their lands on both sides of the Channel, rather than partition. In 1153, they obtained the Treaty of Westminster, by which Stephen was to remain king, but to adopt Henry as his heir, a solution that proved workable, albeit at the expense of Stephen's blood heirs, notably his son Eustace. As a result, when Stephen died, the first of the Angevin (from Anjou) dynasty, Henry II (1154–89), inheriting through a woman, came to the throne, albeit to one that was still armed, tense and disorderly, and not as Henry I had intended. Stephen's reign was dropped from legal memory, and anyone in legal possession on the day of Henry I's death in 1135 was now in rightful possession of their lands. More significantly, the barons who defied him were rapidly brought under control, which was clearly achieved by mid-1152.

PLANTAGENETS
HENRY II

King of England (and only of England) he might be, but England was more tangential to Henry II's dominions than had been the case with William I, and this further affected the parameters and practice of royal itineraries. Aside from inheriting England and Normandy from his mother, and Anjou, Maine and Touraine from his father, Henry obtained control over much of central and south-west France through his marriage to the imperious Eleanor of Aquitaine, the divorced wife of Louis VII. Moreover, he used his dominant position in France, where he spent over three fifths of his time, to make further gains, including the subordination of Brittany. Henry's commitment to his French lands led to an absence that forced the administrative development of England, with royal powers put into commission.

Boldly able to take and use the initiative, Henry sought power and to use the authority he enjoyed. That helped lead to an expansionism in France, Wales, Ireland and Scotland, and to determined opposition to critics within England. Most prominent among these was Thomas Becket, Archbishop of Canterbury. His friendship with Henry gained him the post, but disagreement over the right of clerics to accept trial only in Church courts led the two men to clash, and to the obdurate Becket's eventual murder in 1170 by four of Henry's knights who had taken an angry outburst at face value. Henry had to do penance while Becket, apparently a martyr to cruel kingship, became a saint. The cult of Becket was to be a curse for the medieval English monarchy, but Henry survived the crisis: there was no alternative and he was the legitimate and anointed ruler. As a reminder that religion was part of the lives of monarchs, Henry himself was devoted to Edward the Confessor, canonized in 1161, and to Edmund, King (of East Anglia) and Martyr, who had been killed by the Vikings in 869, bringing his dynasty to a close.

The king also sought to increase royal judicial powers as a means to consolidate English government. Royal writs and royal justices were important to a standardisation of the administration of common law. Moreover, the access of the population to the king's law helped ensure that monarchy, not feudal aristocracy, wielded power, and thus that the authority of the monarchy was less limited by the latter than in France. Yet, at the same time, greater power risked more arbitrary decisions: authority could be used for good or bad, and Henry's arbitrary character meant that he could be an oath-breaker. Indeed, the popularity of Becket in some quarters was a comment on concern about the Crown, concern that was to focus on Henry's second surviving son, John (1199–1216).

A masterful and driving personality, Henry was an angry man in a hurry who lacked the clothing of majesty, but had that of determination. Not interested in pomp, Henry was not bothered by the forms of dignity, but was determined to regain what had been taken from his inheritance and that of Eleanor. His continued travels around his dominions were designed to that end. He had to face foreign foes, but also those within his own family, notably Henry the Younger, who predeceased him without heir in 1183, and who was willing to ally with these foes. A major war, begun in 1173, was brought successfully to an end in 1174, and, two years later, Richard FitzNigel referred to the king as 'the greatest and illustrious ruler of the world'.

In his last years, however, Henry faced division within his family over the inheritance, notably opposition from his son Richard to his plans, opposition that led to conflict between the surviving sons in 1184. The estrangement of King and Queen, one fictionalised in the film *The Lion in Winter*, put strain on the children, and Henry's apparent favour for his youngest, John, did not help. Nor did the skill of Philip II of France, Philip Augustus, in exploiting these tensions and allying with Richard. Henry himself increasingly lacked flexibility, and at the close of his reign, dying aged fifty-six, was forced into an unsatisfactory settlement with Philip and Richard.

Meanwhile, alongside the clear pattern of a kingship with greater administrative capability, as seen in England and Scotland, came the ambiguity of authority present in Wales. There Rhys (d. 1197), ruler of the principality of Deheubarth, was faced by invasions by Henry in person in 1158, 1163 and 1165, but, although these could bring a temporary submission, as in 1163, Henry found the situation intractable and had to accept Rhys's position in 1171. Yet being a powerful and independent sub-king in effect, with control, including over the lesser Welsh rulers of South Wales, in return for doing homage to Henry, was an inherently unstable situation. In turn, Rhys's quarrelsome sons divided his kingdom.

RICHARD I

Receiving the entire inheritance, with nothing left to John, Henry's oldest surviving son, Richard I (1189–99), was a warrior king. As a young man he had fought in France, and as monarch won fame on the Third Crusade, fighting Saladin, not least victory at Arsuf in 1191; imprisoned in Germany on his way back, he was only freed as the result of an enormous ransom. Most of the rest of Richard's reign was spent fighting in France to regain his losses there, and he was killed during a siege. Although born in England, Richard, as king, spent only half a year there during his reign. There was scant logic to Richard's dominions, in part because Henry had failed to create one, which was understandable given the difficulty of the task. Richard had courage and energy but lacked his father's ingenuity. Had he lived longer, Richard might have matured, but there is little sign of this. Henry's relative lack of interest in glory provided him with an independence of response that his son lacked.

The chronicler Ralph of Coggeshall was impressed by Richard's early years as ruler, both his crusading and his rule in England, but then reported a decline. To contemporaries, he pushed royal powers too hard in order to gain money for his wars, as in 1198 when he insisted that charters be renewed under his new seal. Ralph of Coggeshall saw Richard's death as divine punishment, a verdict on the reign that was to be overshadowed by that of John. Indeed, whereas Richard spent little time in England, there is a statue to him flanking Parliament as well as the tale of 'good king Richard' as opposed to 'bad king John'. Richard's tie to the legends of Robin Hood helped each to give legitimacy to the other, and has also ensured hostile film treatments of John.

Richard is buried alongside his parents and his brother John's second wife, in the abbey church at Fontevraud in Touraine. This recent foundation had been developed by the Angevins, notably Eleanor, as a rival to the Capetian family church at Saint Denis near Paris. Eleanor retired to live there in 1200, dying four years later; but Fontevraud was soon to be swept from the family by French conquest.

JOHN

The chroniclers approved of some of the early policies of John (1199–1216), but he was not to prove equal to the challenges of his reign, and, combined with the contingencies leading to, and reflecting, a lack of success, they brought out his weaknesses. A tough and nasty individual, naturally avaricious and suspicious, who lacked skills of man-management and did not improve with adversity, John became instead a repeated practitioner of intimidation – as in 1214 when he went to Bury St Edmunds to bully the monks into electing his favoured candidate as abbot. He entered the chapter house with a sword carried as part of the entry, and threatened the monks with his *odium* (hatred). This was scarcely a peaceful pilgrimage. He was also held responsible for murders, notably of his nephew Arthur in 1203, who possibly was killed while John was drunk. John, moreover, sexually harassed the wives and daughters of his barons. In 1225, a monk of St Albans, a prominent abbey, had a vision in which he saw John in hell tormented by clothes of intolerable weight.

John did not have the personal prestige necessary to retain the support of the nobles. His lack of military prowess was summed up in the epithet 'softsword'. His dispute with Pope Innocent III had led to England being placed under papal interdict in 1208 and John being excommunicated in 1209, but he did not give in until 1213, the interdict ending the following year. Indeed, in 1213, John did homage to Innocent III, making England a papal fief, and in 1215 undertook to go on crusade.

French success in overrunning Normandy and Anjou in 1203–4 led John both to spend far more time in England than his two predecessors, and to focus his efforts in England on raising the resources for *revanche*, only to fail and thus provoke rebellion in England, a situation that was to recur under his son, Henry III. Rebellion led in 1215 to John being forced to accept the terms of Magna Carta, a definition and limitation of royal rights, and one that removed the ability of the Crown to determine these rights. Instead, England was to be a political community headed by the king but to which he could be held accountable. The justice he had not practised was to be forced on him.

John, unsurprisingly, was unwilling to implement the agreement; and this led to a new civil war, albeit one that was to be far shorter than that during Stephen's reign. John's baronial opponents, who had few options, offered the throne to Louis, the son of Philip Augustus of France, while Scotland and Gwynedd turned against John. He also lost much support within England. John died in 1216 while on campaign. His reputation was awash, like much of his baggage train lost in the quicksand and tide of the Wash. Allegations that he was poisoned are questionable. Instead, overeating might have been the cause.

HENRY III

As a nine-year-old, Henry III (1216–72), John's son, crowned in Gloucester, was someone who could be the repository of hopes and expectations, rather than fears. Indeed, rather as James VI of Scotland received frequent instruction about the failings of his mother, Mary, Queen of Scots, Henry was to be repeatedly warned about John's failings and was to commit himself sincerely to Magna Carta. There was no sinisterly ambitious uncle equivalent to the fatal problem Richard III (1483–5) posed to Edward V (1483). Instead, Henry was more akin to Edward VI (1547–53), although without the illness that brought to an end the latter's short reign.

Victory against French forces and supporters in 1217, at Lincoln and off Sandwich, followed by Louis abandoning his claims, owed nothing to Henry, who was crowned for the second time, and more splendidly, at Westminster and with St Edward's crown, in 1220. His piety came to the fore from the 1220s, with pilgrimages to East Anglian holy sites from 1226. However, Henry eventually helped jeopardise the relatively harmonious settlement of domestic differences during his minority by asserting his powers and granting favour to friends and advisers. The issues posed by favourites were to be continual throughout royal history, and had already been seen with earlier kings, notably opposition to Edward the Confessor's Norman protégés.

With favourites, there are the issues raised by any use of a term that is at once seen as pejorative and descriptive. Aside from the extent to which the use of language can be misleading, there are also the problems raised by reading from one episode to another. Moreover, too much of an emphasis can be placed on one side of a past contention. The side that is most hostile to the Crown tends to attract most attention, but that does not necessarily mean that the criticism is the most accurate as a description of what occurred. At any rate, the established elite tended to resist favourites who were not members or who were rivals, the two overlapping to a degree. Henry earned criticism for his favour to his Poitevin half-brothers and the supposedly evil counsel received from aliens was castigated. In his *Chronica Majora* (1236–59), Matthew Paris, a monk at St Albans, complained about the abuses of Henry's court and his foreign favourites.

Again, as a reminder of multiple roles, Matthew Paris was commissioned by Henry to write a new life of Edward the Confessor, whose cult attracted the king. As a major part of his rebuilding of Westminster Abbey, Henry built a new tomb for Edward after whom he named his eldest son. Henry's creation of Westminster Abbey as a coronation church and royal burial place was part and parcel of the process by which Westminster became the physical and ceremonial setting of English monarchy. London and Westminster were to act as a bi-focal capital in a process intended to help the Crown. Moreover, the royal tombs became significant as sites for royal self-representation, as with the inscriptions on the tombs of Edward III and Richard II.

A devoted husband and the father of five children, Henry was pious and ambitious, but lacked persistence and military skill. Relations with many of the barons deteriorated, not least due to different concepts of good kingship. Yet, as with John, failure abroad crucially contributed to the crisis, as military failure against France, notably the loss of Poitou in 1224 and in campaigns of 1230 and 1242, damaged Henry's reputation and finances. His international policy, nevertheless, became bolder. Henry added to his interest in securing German help to regain lands lost to France, a project to conquer Sicily as part of an unsuccessful plan to have his brother, Richard of Cornwall, elected Holy Roman Emperor, and also to forward a crusade. The Treaty of Paris of 1259, however, saw a settlement – one in which Henry accepted his father's failure and that of his own earlier years. Henry renounced the claim to Normandy, Anjou, Maine, and Poitou, while he rendered homage to Louis IX for what was left: Aquitaine.

Royal Anger

'He was absolutely furious . . . And drawing his sword, as if filled with madness, he wished to kill the Justiciar. But the Earl of Chester and others who were there, placing themselves in the way, saved him from death. And he withdrew from the king's presence until the king's anger subsided and calmed down.'

Roger of Wendover, 1229

Royal Indolence

'Good sauce, clear wine, white bread, chambers and tapestries, and the like, to drink, to consult with quibblers, to ride . . . on docile mounts, the king loves better all that than to put on a coat of mail.'

Anonymous writer in circle of Savary de Mauléon, 1230

In England, in order to enforce what they regarded as good kingship, many barons, meanwhile, sought to wrest power out of Henry's hands and curb royal abuses. Initially successful in 1258, they lost power to Henry in 1261, but rebellion followed in 1263 and civil war broke out anew in 1264. In part, this was a clash within the royal family, with Henry opposed by his able and ambitious brother-in-law, Simon de Montfort, Earl of Leicester, but far more was involved. There were issues of principle as well as of patronage. Henry was defeated and captured at Lewes in 1264, but his dynamic eldest son, Edward, revived the royal position, and Simon was defeated and killed at Evesham in 1265. Henry returned to power, but under the shadow of the civil war, rather like Charles II after the Exclusion Crisis of 1679–81.

Praised for piety and a clear demonstration of the role of the king as God's vice-regent, Henry was repeatedly criticised as an inadequate king, lacking judgment and justice in many of his domestic affairs, not least his patronage. He provided domestic peace for decades, but then lost it spectacularly.

A King on Himself

'For the forty-five years, in which, by the will of God and helped by his grace, we have held the government of our kingdom . . . with our utmost desire and all our strength, we have not ceased to study and labour . . . for the peace and tranquillity of each and everyone.'

Henry III, 1261

EDWARD I

Victor at Evesham, Edward I (1272–1307) was a warrior king throughout, which helped ensure that he served as a model for his warrior grandson, Edward III. Born in 1239, he was named by Henry after his patron saint, Edward the Confessor, which broke with the pattern of Norman names for the royal family. Edward soon became a factor in politics and the succession, his 1254 marriage to Eleanor of Castile was part of Henry's attempt to strengthen his position. So also with the establishment of Edward as, in effect, governor of Gascony (Aquitaine) in an attempt to settle disputes over its (and his) future. In a sensible policy, Henry sought to have Edward visit all parts of his appanage (current provision of lands) and he therefore visited Chester and nearby areas of Wales in 1255. In 1258, he accompanied his father on an unsuccessful campaign against Gwynedd, one that brought Henry no respect.

Edward turned toward support for baronial reformers and moved against his father, before backing royal authority in the civil war that began in 1264 in which he played a key role in secur-ing victory. This civil war left him determined to temper kingship with justice, and reform with order. When Edward succeeded his father, he was on crusade, surviving an attempt at assassination that year, and he was to die while campaigning against the Scots.

The peaceful nature of his succession, despite his being abroad, combined with the absence of the coronation, was a prod-uct of the defeat of the barons in 1265. This trouble-free succes-sion after the turmoil of his father's reign illustrated the strength of both the dynasty and the institution of monarchy. Moreover, the new reign began as a fresh start, as had that of Henry in 1216. Impressive as general, ruler, administrator and legislator, Edward was a dominating and durable personality, with more judgment, strength of will and military ability than Henry. A determined monarch, Edward was firm in the defence of his rights, strong, and pre-emptory in the maintenance of his dignity. He continued his father's focus on Westminster where he decorated the Painted Chamber and reconstructed St Stephen's Chapel. A pious Christian dedicated to the Virgin Mary, Edward took the growing anti-Semitism of thirteenth-century warfare so far as to expel the Jewish community in 1290.

Edward's reign was significant for the development of Parliament. In the long term, this was to be transformative and to constrain the power of the Crown, but in the short term, it was designed to help energise England, not least by enabling govern-ment to draw on economic growth. Magna Carta had linked taxa-tion to consent, and this link was taken further in the concept of representation in Parliament, namely a broadening out of what had originated as the king's council of barons. The writs summon-ing representatives of the clergy, counties and boroughs to the 1295 Parliament instructed them to appear with authority to give advice and consent on behalf of the communities for which they spoke. Aside from raising taxation (and Edward was involved in a difficult and costly war with France in 1294–8), Parliament was to serve the need for a national political focus, and be part of the delicate political compact necessary for peace and stability. He might be an autocrat, but Edward was also concerned to get things done. Alongside his management of the higher nobility, this attitude helped ensure compromise and the avoidance of political breakdown; a mission and method, however, that he failed to follow in Scotland.

London and the Crown

London's opposition to John and Henry III underlay much of the attitude of Edward I, who revoked the City's liberties and installed a government under his own officers from 1285 to 1299. Moreover, the Tower of London was greatly strengthened. From then on, London was increasingly the royal capital and not a city following an independent political course. The exceptional power and authority of the Crown in England and its strong centralising tendencies were key factors in London's development. Taking forward its prominent part in favour of Stephen but, later, against John, the city's central role in the overthrow of Edward II in 1326 and Henry VI in 1461 reflected its continuing capacity for pursuing its own course, but it did so as a central part of the kingdom and not as an autonomous city state. Tensions slackened under Edward III.

WALES

Edward cut athwart monarchy elsewhere in Britain. Wales had been divided into a number of principalities but a combination of their problems and rivalries, and, on the other hand, of English pressure led to Llywelyn the Great (d. 1240) and his grandson, Llywelyn ap Gruffydd (d. 1282), uniting native Wales (*pura*

Wallia). Moving away from the earlier practice of taking advice from other Welsh princes, they sought to create a Welsh political unit and single political authority where none had existed before. The two Llywelyns sought to extend overlordship over the other native rulers and to persuade the English crown to accept the homage of the Prince of Gwynedd for the whole of native Wales, the other rulers having done homage to the prince. In 1216, at a sort of parliament or council meeting of Welsh rulers at Aberdyfi, Llywelyn the Great dealt with competing territorial claims within *pura Wallia*. He alone used the title of Prince, and sought to act as the legal overlord of the other Welsh rulers in order to lessen the chance of the king of England meddling in Welsh politics. Borrowing English royal techniques, Llywelyn used great and privy seals. He was also a supporter of the Church, notably the Cistercian monastery of Aberconwy, as well as of the native bards who celebrated his talents, helped unify the laws and encouraged a sense of unity.

Nevertheless, Llywelyn the Great failed to secure the treaty with the English crown necessary to cement his position. The principality he had built up depended entirely on his personality and, unlike England or Scotland, had little institutional framework to sustain it, while stability was threatened by the contested succession.

After conflict, his grandson, Llywelyn, gained sole power in Gwynedd in 1255 and was acknowledged as Prince of Wales by Henry III in 1267 by the Treaty of Montgomery. Llywelyn, however, failed to do homage to Edward I and lacked the ability to define a compromise. The resulting English invasion in 1277 saw Llywelyn driven to surrender, do homage, surrender lands, and accept that the homage of most of the Welsh leaders was transferred to the king. In 1282–3, a renewed invasion led to the death of Llywelyn in a skirmish and Edward established control.

As a result, the Welsh principality was reconceptualised, with the politico-constitutional achievements of the rulers of

Gwynedd serving as a basis for rule by Edward and his succes- sors. The principality recognised in 1267 survived, but, as a dependency of England from 1284, it was not represented in Parliament nor under the English courts. Signs of independ- ence were carefully suppressed. Llywelyn's seals were melted, his silver made into plate, and his princely coronet displayed in Westminster Abbey.

The principality was granted in 1301 to Edward's eldest son, the future Edward II, who was created Prince of Wales and who had been born in Caernarfon Castle in 1285. Although the principality would not be annexed to England until 1536, it was no longer independent, but essentially an honorific, rather than independent, position for the heirs to the English throne.

SCOTLAND

Larger, wealthier and a kingdom, Scotland had followed a differ- ent pattern to that of Wales, but had also lacked the enforced cohesion that was brought to England by the campaigning and conquests of the tenth and eleventh centuries. The area centred on the Moray Firth, a separate kingdom, resisted control until the early twelfth century. Moreover, Galloway was largely autono- mous, while the Hebrides and the Isle of Man remained a sepa- rate lordship under Norway until 1266. So also with Orkney and Shetland until 1468, when they were pledged by Christian I for the payment of the dowry of his daughter Margaret on her betrothal to James III, only for the non-payment of the dowry to lead to their retention. Within the areas of royal control in Scotland, the same processes of development seen in Wessex were influential, not least linkage with the Church. Yet, as far as much of Scotland was concerned, the thirteenth century also saw the conquest and extension of control that Edward I was, differ- ently, to achieve in Wales.

Educated at the court of his brother-in-law Henry I, David I (1124–53) had proved a key developer of Scottish monarchy, showing the importance of being able to introduce new techniques of government, which is not the situation for the modern monarchy. He minted the first Scottish coins, introduced feudal tenures, encouraged immigration by Norman nobles, and organised the central government on the Anglo-Norman pattern. He was also a major patron of the Church.

The Scottish kingdom became strong, and royal warriors extended its authority from the central lowlands. Indeed, a series of able rulers, William the Lion (1165–1214), Alexander II (1214–49) and Alexander III (1249–86), none of whom displayed the weaknesses of John and Henry III, brought control over modern Scotland bar the Orkneys and Shetlands. The formation of a distinctly Scottish Church also contributed to the idea of Scottishness, and broad social, economic and cultural developments to a measure of cohesion.

As so frequently, the luck of birth and death brought vulnerability and strife. Alexander died in 1286, to be succeeded by a young granddaughter, Margaret, the three-year-old Maid of Norway. Edward I saw this as an opportunity to increase his family's power, and in 1289 secured agreement for her marriage to the future Edward II.

The rights and laws of Scotland were to be preserved but the personal union of the Crowns that was to be achieved in 1603 now appeared likely. Margaret, however, died in 1290, leaving a number of claimants. Asked to adjudicate, Edward pressurised the claimants into recognising his overlordship over the Crown of Scotland, before declaring John Balliol king in 1292. Balliol swore fealty and did homage to Edward. English hegemony appeared established and Edward encouraged appeals by Scots to English courts.

In turn, tensions led Edward to invade in 1296, defeating the Scots. Balliol surrendered the kingdom to Edward who styled himself Lord of Scotland, placing the kingdom in abeyance. What this could have led to is unclear, for major rebellions launched in 1297 and 1306 by William Wallace and Robert Bruce respectively led to a contested kingdom, with Bruce having himself crowned Robert I. *Braveheart* (1995), a flawed film (in terms of historical accuracy) about Wallace, provided a very harsh portrayal of the English rulers.

Edward II

The problems posed by any domestic compact between Crown and possible opponents were accentuated under Edward II (1307–27), the fourth son of Edward I; the older three had all died young. He combined political failure with a lack of military ability. Either on its own would have been serious, but the combination produced an acute crisis, one that – if not as serious as that in 1215–17 – served to underline the dependence of monarchy on monarchs. Albeit in a very different context, that remains the situation today. Nevertheless, Edward at least dealt with one major problem by providing for the succession. That he had no children until 1312 was a cause of alarm, but that year he had a son, Edward III, by Isabella, daughter of Philip IV of France, who he had married in 1308. In contrast, her brothers Louis X, Philip V, and Charles IV died without sons in 1316, 1322 and 1328. This led to a contentious succession that caused the Hundred Years War between the two claimants, Philip VI, their cousin, and Edward III, their nephew. Under the Salic Law of succession which operated in France, royal succession could not be through a woman. This would also later ensure that Victoria, on the death of William IV in 1837, could not inherit Hanover, which instead was inherited by a surviving son of George III, her uncle Ernest (1837–51).

Edward II made the difficulties he faced worse as a result of his own incompetence. His inability to deal with the Scots stemmed in part from his quarrels with his barons, notably over the arrogant Piers Gaveston, a Gascon upstart who may have been his lover as well as his brother-in-arms. Edward had learned nothing from the events of his grandfather, Henry III's, reign. Edward I had banished Gaveston, but his son recalled him, made him Earl of Cornwall, and gave him considerable wealth and a prominent role. Edward's favour for Gaveston led to a political crisis with nobles fearing exclusion from influence and in 1311 he was forced to accept Ordinances limiting royal power and exiling Gaveston. Edward, however, recalled him. The nobility reacted vigorously and Gaveston was murdered by the Earl of Warwick in 1312.

An Interim Report

'Our King Edward has now reigned six full years and up until now he has achieved nothing praiseworthy or memorable, except that he has made a splendid marriage and has produced a handsome son and heir to the kingdom.'

Vita Edwardi Secundi, 1313

In 1314, the king suffered the humiliation of a crushing defeat by the Scots at Bannockburn. This was followed by the loss of Stirling Castle and by increasingly bold Scottish raids into England. Edward's wealthy cousin, Thomas, Earl of Lancaster, took effective control of the government in the aftermath of Bannockburn, with Edward obliged to heed the Ordinances.

In turn, Edward, who had fallen out anew with Lancaster in 1319, regained control in England in 1322, defeating his opponents, notably Lancaster who was beheaded. Edward repealed the Ordinances, but his limited ability to learn had been already shown by his support for new favourites, the Despensers, notably Hugh the Younger with whom he was rumoured to have a homosexual relationship. Lancaster's supporters were brutally treated and the Despensers given much wealth. The *Vita Edwardi Secundi* observed in 1325: 'The king's harshness has indeed increased so much today that no one, however great or wise, dares to cross the king's will ... Whatever pleases the king, though lacking in reason, has the force of law.'

In the meanwhile, the expedition against the Scots led by Edward in 1322 had been a dismal failure, and Edward later that year was nearly ambushed by a Scottish raiding party in Yorkshire. A truce with the Scots followed in 1323.

Distrusted and unpopular, Edward failed to conform to contemporary expectations of kingship. Lacking dignity, he had unroyal tastes such as digging ditches and boating, although also the royal one of hunting. Edward's very narrowly based and deeply unpopular regime was rapidly overthrown in 1326 by his wife Isabella and her lover from 1325, Roger Mortimer, who had gone into exile after Lancaster's defeat. They invaded from the Low Countries and Edward's support dissolved. His eldest son was in his mother's camp and was declared Keeper of the Realm. No one was prepared to fight for Edward who was captured. He was then deposed by Parliament, charged with weakness, incompetence, failure and taking evil counsel. Threatened with the exclusion of his family from the succession, Edward agreed to this deposition in January 1327, accepting that he would consent to his subjects' will, although it was then pretended that he had abdicated before his subjects had withdrawn their fealty. This ensured a conservative presentation of the coup, prefiguring the 1689 claim that James II had abdicated.

Edward was murdered in Berkeley Castle later that year, supposedly with a red-hot poker inserted in his anus to leave few obvious incriminating marks on his body. Other than Bannockburn, this fate tends to be the detail most remembered about Edward, which is an instructive comment on history. In fact, this detail was not much noted in subsequent decades and it is unclear how Edward was murdered, although it was obviously done in order to prevent attempts to free the king. A contemporary chronicler, the *Brut*, had Lancaster's ally, Humphrey, 4th Earl of Hereford, killed at the battle of Boroughbridge in 1322 by a pikeman hiding underneath a bridge through which he thrust his pike into the earl's anus.

Replaying History

John, 3rd Earl of Bute, the key advisor of George III, was wrongly rumoured to be the lover of George's mother Augusta. A comparison with Roger Mortimer was to be developed in the opposition newspaper the *Monitor*, on 9 October 1762, and in the published version of the 1763 play *The Fall of Mortimer*.

Edward III

Isabella and Mortimer ruled arbitrarily for the first years of the young Edward III (1327–77), who had been born in 1312. Humiliated and understandably resentful, Edward staged a coup in 1330. A council was meeting in Nottingham, and Edward and a small group of friends boldly and successfully entered the castle through an underground passage. Mortimer was seized, tried in Parliament and hanged, while Isabella was confined in Castle Rising; Edward ruled now as king without his earlier dependence on the pair.

Edward brought political stability after the chaos of Edward II's reign, a considerable achievement. Edward's magic formula was to bind the nobility to him in pursuit of successful foreign war, although that was later to lead to hostile comparisons. Thus, on 29 August 1752, the Tory (opposition) newspaper *Old England* took aim at the Hanoverian interests of George II and the

Continental interventionism of his British ministers in the person of Edward: 'the grand fault of his reign was the unhappy passion he indulged to foreign acquisitions,' and that he too realised 'that an island cannot extend itself beyond the waves which confine it. Britain he found was to be enriched but not extended.'

Edward possessed the ability and determination to restore royal prestige and authority, to avenge his father's humiliations, and to reassert the position of his dynasty in France. He was also far more successfully and happily married than his father, Philippa of Hainault proving the very opposite to Isabella and providing him with twelve children. Notably effective in his dealing with the barons, Edward brought many into his circle as Knights of the Order of the Garter, which he established in 1348.

This was an aspect of Edward's use of the Arthurian legend to add the authority of age to his deeply felt but also character-istically showy embrace of chivalric ideas, as was seen with the foundation of the College of St George to serve the royal chapel in Windsor Castle, where Edward had been born. Hitherto dedicated to Saint Edward the Confessor, this chapel was re-dedicated to St George, whom Edward III chose as the patron saint for the Order, thus fixing providential support by a form of white magic. George was a more martial figure than the existing national saints, Edmund the Martyr and Edward the Confessor, and in 1351 was acclaimed as patron saint of the English. With his powerful sense of honour, Edward liked to look to the example of the saint. In another break with the Confessor, Edward was the first to have a number formally included in his official title, and that was 'King Edward the Third after the Conquest', which left out the Confessor as a pre-Conquest monarch.

Edward's political formula seriously broke down in his later years when the recovery of France under Charles V (1364–80) combined with a political vacuum in England in the king's dotage and an upsurge in factionalism. Edward was unable to maintain his 1360 peace with France. The problems of his later years were serious, but his poor response contributed greatly to difficulties. Increasingly unwell, Edward may have suffered mentally from the effects of a series of strokes. His extravagant and unpopular mistress, Alice Perrers, served as a focus for tension, but the real problem was that there was little precedent to help with the problem created by an old and ailing monarch, and certainly not the regency provisions that were to be shown with George III. The problems of the last years of Henry II and, even more, Henry III, were not an encouraging example. Edward's popular wife, Philippa of Hainault, with whom he had a close and loving marriage, had died in 1369. The couple was a potent symbol: in 1842, Victoria and Albert dressed as Philippa and Edward for a fancy-dress ball hosted at Buckingham Palace.

Paradoxically, however, although the problems of longevity were readily apparent, the succession was clear. Edward's oldest son, Edward, the Black Prince, brave victor over the French at Poitiers in 1356, predeceased his father, dying in 1376, one of a number of heirs that did so across Britain's royal history. Nevertheless, there was an incontestable successor in the person of Edward's grandson, Richard.

In Scotland, in contrast, the situation was difficult. The Bruce family provided successive monarchs, but Robert I's infant son, David II (1329–71), was challenged from 1322 by Edward Balliol, who enjoyed the support of Edward III who, in 1334, restored him to the throne. Balliol was driven out in 1332 and 1334, but Edward repeatedly invaded. David, an exile under the protection of Philip VI of France in 1334–41, invaded England in order to help the French in 1346, only to be defeated at Neville's Cross near Durham, taken prisoner, and held captive until 1357, when Edward made peace. The difficulties of the task, combined with Edward's focus on France, ensured that the English could not establish control over Scotland in the shape of a subordinate king, or even annex Lothian.

Commemorating a King

Inscription on the Purbeck marble tomb of Edward III in Westminster Abbey:

'Here is the glory of the English, the paragon of past kings, the model of future kings, a merciful king, the peace of the peoples, Edward the third fulfilling the jubilee of his reign, the unconquered leopard, powerful in war like a Maccabee. While he lived prosperously, his realm lived again in honesty. He ruled mightily in arms; now in Heaven let him be a king.'

IRELAND

Ireland also saw military facts counter political possibilities. Anglo-Norman forces under Richard of Clare, 'Strongbow', invaded in 1169 and rapidly seized much of Ireland, in part with Irish support as in the 1170 defeat of the Norse king of Dublin, who was a product of the Viking diaspora. Henry II arrived in 1171 in order to establish his rights in accordance with the Papal Bull of 1155. Henry imposed his authority on his barons and obtained the submission of many of the Irish kings and of the Irish Church. In 1175, by the Treaty of Windsor, Henry II was recognised as Lord of Ireland, a title implying overlordship over the petty kings, but leaving somewhat ambiguous the position of Rory O'Connor, the Irish High King.

Much of Ireland, however, was under only limited English control and, in the 1310s, Scottish intervention added a new qualification to this position. The possibility of a Scottish conquest was ended by defeat at Faughart in 1318, with Robert I's brother Edward, who had been crowned High King in 1316, killed. However, a Gaelic resurgence limited direct English control to the Pale, the area around Dublin. English intervention continued, but the expedition by Richard II in 1399 was the last by an English king until William III successfully invaded in 1690. Richard's expedition was to be the last hurrah of a reign heading for disaster.

RICHARD II

Wilful and no warrior, the young Richard (1377–99), born in 1367, lacked personal prestige and fortitude, and some of the lords saw his youth as limiting his fitness to rule. He survived the Peasants' Revolt of 1381, which, in many respects, was an attempt to pressure him into changes of policy that would accord with the peasants' concept of good kingship. After London had been occupied and unpopular ministers murdered, Richard met the main body of the rebels under Wat Tyler at Smithfield, just outside the city walls. During the meeting, William Walworth, Mayor of London, believing that Tyler was threatening Richard, lunged forward and stabbed him in the neck, whereupon one of the king's knights dispatched Tyler with a sword through the stomach. Astutely, Richard averted further violence by promising to be the rebels' leader. The peasants returned home. This, however, was not to be a Becket moment. The context and circumstances were totally different. Richard revoked his promise and the surviving leaders were then hunted down, Henry Bolingbroke, the future Henry IV, a cousin of Richard's, being one of those entrusted with restoring order.

At the level of the aristocracy, the issue of favourites led to bitter criticism, with conflict and judicial murders as a result in the late 1380s. Finding him untrustworthy, Richard's opponents feared for their lives, and there was a brief civil war, or rather campaign, in 1387 with the Royalists defeated at Radcot Bridge. The victorious rebellious nobles, the Appellants, tried their opponents for treason in the Merciless Parliament the following year. With great brutality, Royalists were killed in London with popular support, Richard's efforts to save his friends being unavailing. The judicial and extra-judicial murders ended with Parliament granting pardons to the Appellants and with a formal reknitting of monarchy: in Westminster Abbey, during a high mass, Richard repeated his coronation oath and the peers their oaths of homage.

Richard was obliged to accept dominance by the Appellants until, in 1389, he took personal charge of government and dismissed them. Tension eased in the early 1390s and royal control of government increased, but both remained an issue, seen for example when in 1394, an angry Richard struck the Earl of Arundel unconscious with an usher's baton: he had turned up late for the funeral of the queen, Anne of Bohemia.

Richard's narcissism helped make him wilful, violent, unpredictable, unable to take criticism and detached from reality. His flawed personality matched a policy drawing on the model of the French monarchy, one focused on the need for obedience to a magisterial Crown. For magnificence, he rebuilt Westminster Hall and commissioned Hugh Herland's timber roof, a work of dramatic scale. In some respects, Richard's stance prefigured the views associated with Henry VIII and later James I and Charles I; but Richard certainly lacked Henry's ability, drive and good fortune. He could show Henry's petulant ruthlessness, but not his shrewdness.

Richard pursued competitive status with the rulers of France who based their claims to obedience on the sacramental quality of the French monarchy, the use at coronations of the holy oil used by St Remi for the anointing of Clovis at Reims, which miraculously reproduced itself. No monarchy in Europe could compete with it, which was why the use at Henry IV's coronation for the first time of the holy oil reputedly given to Becket was so important. It represented an attempt to boost the sacramental claims of the English monarchy. Henry IV was not the innovator. It was Richard who had discovered the ampule in the Tower of London and asked to be anointed again with it, only for Archbishop Arundel to refuse on the grounds that he could only be anointed once. So it was left to Henry to use. Similarly, the closed imperial crown which Froissart claimed was used at Henry's coronation must also have been a creation of Richard's.

Alongside the grandiose aspects of Richard's kingship, there were actions seen by some as tyrannical, including the extortion of forced loans and blank charters from people who were terrorised by his retinue of Cheshire guards. It is unclear how far this view about tyranny was widespread among contemporaries, rather than being a judgment of later Lancastrian commentators. Richard saw himself as helping lesser members of society, but much that he was associated with had also been seen with John and Edward II, and had brought both opposition.

There were also tensions within the royal family, with Richard's lack of an heir from his two marriages, to Anne of Bohemia and the six-year-old Isabella of Valois, making him uneasy about the attitudes of his uncles and cousins. In turn, his policies helped make them more hostile. As Richard exerted more power in the late 1390s, one of the uncles, Thomas, Duke of Gloucester, was murdered in 1397, while, in 1399, Richard unnecessarily deprived his distrusted cousin Henry Bolingbroke of his inheritance – a foolish step.

Bolingbroke returned from exile that year, while Richard was away in Ireland. This was a crisis different to that leading to Edward II's removal in 1326. There was a clearer breakdown in relations between the king and great lords troubled by the direction of royal attitudes, a group that in 1399 included Edward's last surviving son, Edmund of Langley. Richard's absolutist aspirations were also made more difficult as a result of the protracted economic crisis of the century-and-a-half following the Black Death which savagely hit Britain in 1348–51. This crisis also put pressure on aristocratic finances.

Richard the Redeless (ill-advised)

'Now, Richard the Redeless, take pity on yourself, you who led your life lawlessly and your people as well . . . covetousness has crushed your crown forever.'

Anonymous poem of 1399

Returning from Ireland, the distrusted Richard was outmanoeuvred, seized, made to abdicate, and imprisoned. Richard's unpopularity and political folly had left him with an overly small power base, a situation that prefigured that of Richard III in 1485. In both cases, too few people had an interest in preserving the regime, and too many an interest in ending it. Moreover, unlike with Richard III and the future Henry VII, the childless and beardless Richard II, whose campaign into Scotland in 1385 and campaigning in Ireland had been singularly unsuccessful, was seen as less martial and manly than the purposeful and bearded future Henry IV. Henry had served as a crusader in the Baltic in 1390–1, winning prestige as a consequence, had six children and was a jousting champion; in a sermon in September 1399, at the Deposition Parliament, Archbishop Arundel portrayed Richard as a boy (*puér*) and Bolingbroke as a man (*vir*), even though they were the same age. This was also a warning against boy kings such as a possible Yorkist claimant, Edmund, 5th Earl of March (1391–1425), a great-great-grandson of Edward III who was to be a loyal vassal of the Lancastrians: his claim was through Edward's second surviving son.

Bolingbroke had mounted a military challenge, but he won the throne without a battle, like William III in 1688 and, very indirectly, Charles II in 1660, but as neither Edward IV (in 1461 and 1471) nor Henry VII (in 1485) were to do. Like James II in 1688, Richard II lacked resolution in his decisive crisis. In this struggle, indeed, he did not show the decisiveness and courage Richard III was to do in 1485.

Royalty Learns the Kings: A Precis

In 1751, Prince Edward, afterward Duke of York, brother of the future George III, sent Simon, 1st Earl Harcourt, the head of the household for Edward and George, a series of letters that showed how history was presented in terms of royal lives and 'lessons' that could be learned:

'I read this morning part of the life of King John, and must say, that though a king, he was a very sad fellow in private as well as public life . . . [Henry III] did not pursue wise and good measures . . . whose life is very long, and I think very tedious . . . Richard the Second, whose reign I both detest and abhor; firstly, because he gave himself up totally to his flatters; and, secondly, because he had not the least grain of honour.'

Surrendering, Richard had promised to abdicate if his life was spared. Accused of violation of his coronation oath, perjury, undermining liberties, acting as if 'the laws were in his mouth, or in his breast', and therefore tyrannical, he was formally deposed in Parliament. Twelve days later, Henry IV was crowned, after an all-night vigil and a purifying bath. The coronation was held on the anniversary of the Translation of Edward the Confessor, an affirmation of legitimacy.

The coup reflected and accentuated the long-lasting dynastic and political problems that were to be created from rivalries between the numerous descendants of Edward III. The Dukes of Lancaster and York were key cadet (junior) lines of the ruling Plantagenet house, Henry being the son of John of Gaunt, who was the third son of Edward III. Too many children could be as much of a problem as too few. The Ottoman (Turkish) practice of executing siblings, as was done, for example, by Selim I, 'the Grim', in 1512, a practice also seen in the Mughal imperial family in the mid-seventeenth century, was not practical in a Christian society.

In 1400, Richard, then imprisoned in Pontefract Castle, died. He was probably murdered, indeed starved to death, in order to prevent him from acting as a focus for opposition, although he may have chosen to refuse all food. In the 'Epiphany Rising', Richard's supporters had already tried to assassinate Henry in Windsor Castle, but they were betrayed and, variously, lynched by the people or beheaded at Henry's behest.

Punished for Treason

'[C]hopped up like the carcasses of beasts killed in the chase [hunting], partly in sacks and partly on poles slung across pairs of men's shoulders, where they were later salted to preserve them [for display].'

Adam Usk on some of those drawn, hanged, beheaded and quartered for treason, 1400

LATER MEDIEVAL SCOTLAND

The wars of independence (1296–1357) secured the independence and territorial integrity of Scotland, and this success helped develop a sense of national consciousness. A distinct Scottish ecclesiastical province was created by the Lateran Council of 1215. John Barbour's poem, the *Brus*, composed in Scots in 1375, was an anti-English national epic centring on Robert the Bruce and the 'freedom' of Scotland he had secured. Scotland's identity was defined by opposition to England.

The fate of monarchy in Scotland provided an instructive parallel to that in England. Abler than Richard II, Robert Stewart, who succeeded his childless uncle, David II, in 1371, was more astute than Richard in his dealings with the magnates, possibly because he was himself a magnate. Robert used his children to establish marital links, including with the MacDonald Lord of the Isles.

Two rival factions within the royal family, however, competed for control from 1384 when Robert II (1371–90) became too ill to reign. This led to much instability and violence. Robert's son, Robert III (1390–1406), was less fortunate than his father, in large part because of divisions within the royal family, especially between his eldest son, David, and his brother, Robert, Duke of Albany. David was seized in 1402 and died in captivity. However, these disputes did not initially lead to a civil war. Robert III's surviving son, James I (1406–37), was captured by the English while en route to France as a child, and was held for nineteen years, before being returned in 1424. James only gained power in 1425 by bringing down the former regent, Murdac, 2nd Duke of Albany; son of the duke who had dominated the last years of Robert III. Albany and his relatives were seized and beheaded. James then reimposed royal control in the Highlands, summoned a parliament in Inverness in 1427, executed recalcitrant chiefs, and strengthened royal power. In 1429 and 1431, however, James had to campaign against the Lord of the Isles in the Highlands. James was murdered in his bedchamber in an attempted coup in 1437.

James II (1437–60) faced civil war between aristocratic factions during the 1440s. This was the politics of kidnappings and sudden executions, such as those of the members of the faction of Sir Alexander Livingstone in 1450. Like England, Scotland was a violent society with blood-feuds. In addition, the Scottish rulers were confronted with the issue of dominance over extensive peripheral regions to an extent far greater than in England. This issue had already been a major theme, but during the wars of independence powerful magnates, such as the Earls of Douglas in the Borders, had increased their possessions and power, and this restricted royal authority. Indeed, Archibald, the 4th Earl, sought to seize the future James I in 1406. The MacDonalds, Lords of the Isles and Earls of Ross, were similarly strong in west-coast Scotland. Their title to the Earldom of Ross had been established by force.

Yet, in 1452–5, James II was able to crush the main branch of the Douglases. He personally stabbed William, 8th Earl of Douglas, to death in 1452 while the earl was under the king's safe-conduct. In 1455, the Douglas castle at Threave surrendered in the face of a 'great bombard [cannon]'. In 1476 James III (1460–88) gained Ross and, in 1493, James IV (1488–1513) destroyed the MacDonalds' position and extended his authority to the Hebrides. These gains were achieved with the help of most nobles. They did not see the kings as threats to their position, and it can be misleading to focus on those who did. Much of the opposition, as in England, indeed was from within the royal family.

It would be mistaken to exaggerate Scotland's political success. Its monarchs confronted serious political challenges. James III faced aristocratic opposition from 1479 led by his royal brothers, as well as significant criticism from Parliament. Nevertheless, in 1479, his brother, Alexander, Duke of Albany, was forced to flee to France, and his attempt to regain power, with English help, as Alexander IV in 1482, ultimately failed. James, however, failed to build up support or to keep the magnates sweet. In 1488, unable to muster sufficient support, he was killed shortly after his defeat at Sauchieburn at the hands of a rebel force under the standard of his own son, then still a minor. The rebels took over the government, and, in turn, had to face rebellion in 1489. Given such problems at the centre, the stress on local control of much administration was prudent as well as necessary.

Yet in Scotland, as in England, the striking feature of most fifteenth-century violence was the attempt to seize control of the central government, generally in the person of the monarch, and not any drive to create a new polity. As in England, the calibre of the monarch, and his ability to take command of a political situation made complex by competing factions, was important. Political instability essentially arose not from challenges to the power of the state, but rather from the emergence of two rival factions within the royal family. There was no doubt of the integrity of the state, and this national political consciousness was fortified by the frequency with which Parliament met in Scotland. James IV indeed substantially increased the royal revenues, remained popular and brought considerable harmony to Scottish politics, although he used his position to follow an ultimately unsuccessful attempt to increase his international standing. There was also a renaissance of the Scottish court under James IV and James V. James IV spent heavily on beginning Holyrood Palace as a grand residence in Edinburgh.

Henry IV

England was far wealthier than Scotland, but neither wealth nor institutional development prevented instability focused on the personal position of the monarch. Instead, the latter provided a different focus for this instability, one that was to be more fully developed in the seventeenth century.

The brutal end of the Plantagenet line had been eased by a show of legality: Richard had resigned the Crown, and Henry was persuaded not to claim it by right of conquest but by inheritance from Edward III. Parliament, moreover, played a major role in the transfer of the Crown, providing a form of validation. Nevertheless, the removal of Richard, like the earlier crises of his reign, was a proof of the instability produced by royal claims to exercise the prerogative as the monarch thought fit and for the benefit of those he wished to patronise, and the claims of some of the magnates to ensure that they were consulted. Richard's unwillingness to search for compromise ensured that the throne itself was the subject of contention, and this became normative. Yet, claims to the throne still came from within the royal family, as with the removal of Edward II to make way for a government claiming to rule on behalf of his heir. Earlier opposition to Edward II was led by his cousin, Thomas of Lancaster. Henry did not have as clear a claim to the throne as Edward III in 1327, but Richard II's childlessness eased the situation.

Much of Henry's reign was devoted to consolidating his position in England and also in Wales, where there was a major rebellion. The latter was suppressed, as was opposition in England, but there was no opportunity to restore the English position in France. Nor was there an attempt to revive Edward III's intervention in Scotland with which relations were eased when Henry was able to take possession of the heir to the throne, the future James I, who was captured by English pirates in 1406.

War can always go in a different direction, and notably so at Shrewsbury in 1403 when Henry defeated and killed a former ally, the bellicose Percy heir, 'Hotspur', Sir Henry Percy, whose father, Henry, 1st Earl of Northumberland, in turn, was defeated and killed on Bramham Moor in 1408. Henry IV led his forces north, but Northumberland was defeated before he arrived. The earl had played a major role in the overthrow of Richard. The fate of the Percys and their allies illustrated the stakes of politics, but also the degree to which the king was scarcely outside the ambit of deadly violence, not least because of his own usurpation of the throne. This warfare overshadowed the reign and was a background to the steady and brutal punishment of those making treasonable remarks.

But, looked at differently, the warfare represented the consolidation of the new Lancastrian house, a consolidation that, while difficult, proved less so than it was to be for the Yorkist dynasty in 1460–71, although far more so than for the Tudors in 1485–7 or for the Stuarts in 1603. Henry was also lucky and skilful in foreign policy, benefiting from French and Scottish weaknesses, including conflict in France between the leading aristocrats.

The king showed himself skilful in his handling of others, and necessarily wary. He was devout, interested in chivalry, and had a successful first marriage to Mary de Bohun, an aristocratic heiress, who died before he became king. His second marriage, to Joan of Navarre, was also a success, with signs of affection and mutual interests. She was a good stepmother to his children. Henry proved a far more successful manager of Parliament than either Edward III in his later years or Richard II. Henry might be thought a usurper, but he was no tyrant, and proved reasonably successful in restoring Edward's early harmony with the nobility. The manner of his succession helped ensure that not all were encompassed in that harmony, but the situation was far better than had been the case in the meantime. Henry's success also contributed to the domestic stability of England during the reign of Henry V. Henry IV appears to have liked music, certainly as far as the Chapel Royal was concerned, and was the first English ruler known to have selected a Keeper of the King's Books. Henry himself owned a silver bookmark, and had a study where his books were kept.

At the personal level, however, Henry had a bleaker life. Born in 1367, he was the fifth child of John of Gaunt, Duke of Lancaster, but his two elder brothers were already dead and the other two children were girls. His loving first wife died aged twenty-five, giving birth to her sixth child. His mother had died in childbirth aged 21, having borne six children: she had been married for nine years. Henry had a skin disease, possibly psoriasis (though people at the time thought it might be leprosy) episodically from 1387, and from 1406 he had a series of serious problems, possibly a prolapsed rectum, a coronary thrombosis, and gangrenous ulcers. Willpower and faith would have been required to keep going through these problems, and his last words were to ask God to have mercy on him.

Henry was buried in Canterbury Cathedral on the opposite side of the ambulatory from the Black Prince, and close to the shrine of Becket, a mark of his association with the cult of Becket. In turn, Henry V was buried in Westminster Abbey, but Henry VI first in Chertsey Abbey and then in St George's Chapel, Windsor.

WALES IN THE LATER MIDDLE AGES

A separate Welsh royal identity remained on the margins. Between 1369 and 1378 Owain ap Thomas ap Rhodri, or, as the French called him, Yvain de Galles, the great-nephew of Llywelyn ap Gruffudd and the last heir of the Gwynedd dynasty, was active in French service. In 1369 and 1372 there were abortive expeditions to Wales and he was assassinated by an English agent in France in 1378. More seriously, the rising of Owain Glyndŵr (Owen Glendower) in 1400–8 was an indication of the extent of disaffection, and of the survival of separatist feeling in Wales. Yet Glyndŵr's earlier career testified to the process of accommodation. An important landowner, as a young man he was a squire to the Earl of Arundel and in 1385 he took part in Richard II's Scottish campaign.

As a reminder that context was crucial for would-be rulers, Glyndŵr's revolt was in some ways a reaction to the successive crises of the fourteenth century, including the Black Death, but it was also a protest by the leaders of the native community at their neglect by the authorities. Proclaiming himself Prince of Wales in 1400, Glyndŵr rose in North Wales, helped by dissatisfaction with the financial demands of English landowners, and he captured most of South Wales in 1403. As an instance of the crucial interrelationship between would-be rulers and the international context, one that was to be seen repeatedly in England during the Wars of the Roses, Glyndŵr sealed a treaty of alliance with the French, who promised assistance, and he sought to organise regular government, as well as an independent church and universities. A Welsh Parliament was summoned at Machynlleth.

In 1405 Glyndŵr agreed the Tripartite Indenture with Edmund Mortimer and Henry, Earl of Northumberland, by which they were to depose Henry IV and divide England. Glyndŵr's share included, besides Wales, England west of a line from the Mersey to the source of the Trent and then to the Severn just north of Worcester. In contrast, Henry IV had refused to negotiate with Glyndŵr. That year, Glyndŵr, with French help, advanced as far as Worcester, but then withdrew. Henry IV led his forces on campaign in 1400, 1401, 1402, 1403 and 1405, while in 1406 his vigorous son Prince Hal, later Henry V, who had been made King's Lieutenant in 1403, began to inflict serious defeats on the Welsh. Support for the rebellion ebbed and the English were increasingly successful. Glyndŵr himself disappeared in 1415.

He has recently served as a potent symbol of Welsh nationalism, and is certainly more appropriate than the princely house of Gwynedd, whose members, albeit through necessity, spent much of their energy fighting each other and other Welsh rulers. There was, however, a strong opposition to Glyndŵr among some native gentry too; they saw alliance with the English Crown as the best way to maintain their privileges. Glyndŵr was a warrior of his times, who used devastation without remorse, but Prince Hal also brought widespread destruction.

More significantly, Glyndŵr was leading his followers towards a dead end. English power was such that it was only during periods of English civil conflict, such as the Percy rising of 1403, and, earlier, the civil war of Stephen's reign and the crisis at the end of John's reign, that it was possible for Welsh opponents to make much headway. Had Glyndŵr been more successful, it would have exposed Wales to decades of incessant conflict and the Welsh to deep divisions. Like many leaders, for example William Wallace for the Scots, he was more useful as a dead symbol for posterity.

Henry V

Conspiracy and war were both seen under Henry's young and energetic warrior successor, Henry V (1413–22), who had been born in Monnouth Castle in 1386. In 1414, he crushed a conspiracy organised by Sir John Oldcastle, a member of the heretical Lollard tendency that in hindsight was to be seen as anticipating aspects of Protestantism. The following year, on the eve of Henry's invasion of France, the Southampton Plot, a conspiracy to overthrow him in favour of the Earl of March, was betrayed to Henry by March himself, who was being deployed by his brother-in-law, Richard, Earl of Cambridge, the son of Edward III's fourth son, Edmund, Duke of York. Cambridge was beheaded. His son, Richard, 3rd Duke of York, was to rebel against Henry VI, and was also beheaded.

Henry sought to revive the claim of his great-grandfather, Edward III, to the French throne. Prestige was very important. There was the sense of a great tradition to be maintained by campaigning in France and of fame to be gained, as a way to demonstrate warrior virtues and the kingly attributes, as well as manliness. Success would also help to legitimate the new dynasty. Henry's fame was won by beating a far larger French army that year at Agincourt.

Repeated success, notably the conquest of Normandy, led in 1420 to the Treaty of Troyes in which the weak Charles VI betrothed his daughter Catherine to Henry, who was to inherit France on Charles's death and to be regent in the meantime. Such a union was common enough at the time, being seen in the union of the kingdoms of Denmark, Sweden, and Norway in the Union of Kalmar of 1397–1523. It was also to be seen in the unions of Aragon and Castile, Poland and Lithuania, and England and Scotland. The highly impressive Henry might indeed have created a new Anglo-French polity, although asserting control over the whole of France was a formidable task.

An Approachable King?

Shakespeare was mistaken in presenting Henry V as an attractive, approachable individual, for kings were not accessible to their subjects in the manner depicted. At the same time, it was significant that such a presentation could and should be made. Shakespeare captured not so much a degree of domestication in the image of monarchy, for that did not occur, but rather the character envisaged for knightly society and a presentation designed to encompass the whole army. Shakespeare also has Henry repeatedly give due thanks to God, and thus linked Providence to national success. This approach, that of not attributing success to himself, is shown as an aspect of Henry's self-mastery, which was presented as a sign of true manliness and of appropriate kingship. Agincourt was also the subject of the heroic 'Ballad of Agincourt' by Michael Drayton that was first printed in his *Poems Lyric and Pastoral* (1605).

Henry's quest for France caused anxiety in Parliament where there was a fear of becoming a satellite of the more populous France. Indeed, in 1421, the House of Commons approved a petition that the Crowns of England and France should in perpetuity remain separate and independent. In contrast, Henry wanted both to be accepted by the French as a ruler, not conqueror, and also sought the leadership of Christendom.

Charles's son, later Charles VII (1422–61), rejected the treaty, and the war continued, but with Henry's position strengthened by the birth of an heir in 1421. He could defeat the French but not disease, in his case a fatal intestinal condition from which he died on 31 August 1422 in the castle of Vincennes near Paris. Henry was thirty-five. He was buried as he had specified, close to the tomb of Edward the Confessor in Westminster Abbey, to which he had given a significant donation for the rebuilding of the nave. His will ensured that a chantry chapel was constructed there. He had bequeathed to it the large cross he had on the altar in his own chapel. Henry, a man of great energy and effort to the end, was a pious warrior, both in accordance with the conventions of the age and as he lived his life. This element is apt to be underplayed in modern non-academic portrayals of medieval (and later) monarchy.

HENRY VI

His death left a nine-month-old son to become king of England as Henry VI (1422–61, 1470–1), following later in 1422 as king of France on the death of his grandfather, Charles VI, while Henry V's brother, John, Duke of Bedford, became Regent in France, and another uncle, Humphrey, Protector in England. Minorities were periods of difficulty, but that of Henry III had shown that they did not have to lead to political breakdown. Indeed, with both Henry III and Henry VI that did not occur until both men were adults and able, with disastrous consequences, to choose their own advisors and policies.

Henry was crowned king of France in Paris in 1430, but the revival of the French resistance associated initially with Joan of Arc led to the failure of his cause. His major ally, the Duke of Burgundy, changed sides in 1435, Normandy and Gascony were lost in 1449–51, and an English counteroffensive was crushed in 1453.

This represented an appalling collapse in fortune and prestige, and just as John and Henry III had been affected in England by this collapse, so also with Henry VI. Moreover, the contrast with his father was brutally obvious. Henry VI's piety did not bridge the gap, although it left his foundation of Eton College, which was crucial to his liturgical conception of kingship and very close to Windsor. The chapel he planned there was enormous, almost megalomaniac, and if only half was ever built, that was big enough. The twin foundation of King's College, Cambridge was completed, albeit a century later.

Henry VI was a poor leader, incompetent, ineffectual and of questionable stability. He lacked the vigour and success that had enabled his two predecessors to overcome the weak Lancastrian claim. Moreover, in Richard, 3rd Duke of York, descended through his mother from Edward III's second surviving son, Lionel, Duke of Clarence, Henry (descended from the third surviving son, John of Gaunt) faced a determined exponent of a rival and better dynastic claim. The number of peers of the royal blood was a problem. York was a member of the royal family who felt that his status entitled him to more recognition. Later, when Henry, Duke of Cumberland, married a commoner in 1771, his brother, the outraged and overwrought George III, informed another brother, William, Duke of Gloucester, that such a step might threaten civil war, as he claimed that the Wars of the Roses owed much to the intermarriage of Crown and nobility. Like Richard II, Henry was not up to the task of kingship, and the contrast was striking between each and the heroic image, political adroitness, and skilful determination of Richard's father, the Black Prince, and Henry's father, Henry V, respectively.

Adding to this was Henry's stance in the always difficult relationships with, and between, nobles. His partisanship in disputes compromised his royal status so that he could not provide unity among the nobles. Moreover, his wife, Margaret of Anjou, was a determined supporter of faction. Henry was unable to intervene intelligently in disputes between aristocrats. Most notably, the chaos that descended upon northern England in the 1440s was largely due to Henry promoting the Percys at the expense of the Nevilles in Cumberland, and quite unnecessarily so. Henry VI's position was weakened by his inability to establish unity among the nobility, but so was York's. More generally, Henry, who did not know what advice to take, or how best to take it, was apt to mess up sensible arrangements made for him by intelligent subordinates.

Fighting began in the 1450s, with Cade's Rebellion in Kent in 1450, in the face of which, despite attempts by the Lord Mayor to persuade him to stay, Henry had fled London. This was an unimpressive response, contrasting with that of Richard II in the face of the Peasants' Revolt of 1381, and one that helped inspire subsequent Yorkist sympathies in London. Subsequently, in 1453, Henry's mental and physical collapse led to York, the heir presumptive, being made Protector. However, the birth in 1453 of a son to Margaret – Edward, Prince of Wales – ruled out York's chances of succeeding by hereditary right.

In turn, the king's far-from-total recovery from mental illness in the winter of 1454–5 gave the court party, under Edmund, 2nd Duke of Somerset, the opportunity to turn against York. In 1455, at the battle of St Albans, York clashed with Somerset, with the Yorkists picking off their rivals in a series of group assassinations. Somerset was killed and Henry was captured. York lost control of the government in 1457 and fighting then gathered pace. Henry IV had crushed rebellions and Henry V thwarted conspiracies but Henry VI was unable to suppress opposition and indeed was unmanly in contemporary views. He was mentally ill, at least in having a number of breakdowns from 1453. This may have been a genetically linked condition also seen with his grandfather, Charles VI of France. Henry certainly could not cope with crises. Moreover, unlike Prince Hal (later Henry V) during the reign of Henry IV, Henry VI's son and heir Edward, Prince of Wales, was an infant as was to be Edward IV's son and heir, Edward V, the elder of the so-called Princes in the Tower.

The crisis of the 1450s moved from a political confrontation to a dynastic struggle, in large part due to the highly partisan York, who sought to force his way to power when his scheming failed. At the battle of Northampton in July 1460, the Lancastrians were defeated, several of their leaders were killed, and Henry was captured again.

Northampton, however, was not a repetition of St Albans. Having hitherto professed his loyalty to Henry, York now transformed the situation by claiming the throne. This was very much the last resort after a decade in which he had been politically marginalised by those round Henry, but it was also a breach in the settled order. Margaret of Anjou, who had escaped from Northampton, was not prepared to see the disinheritance of her son Edward, and the Lancastrians attacked, defeated and killed York at Wakefield in December 1460. His severed head, adorned with a paper crown, was displayed on the gate of York. This did not end the Yorkist claim on the throne because York's ambitious and energetic eighteen-year-old son Edward then claimed the throne as Edward IV. 1461 saw the Lancastrians victorious at St Albans in February, with Henry then freed, but subsequently heavily defeated at Towton in March, and this firmly established Edward's position on the throne. Towton may have involved as many as 60,000 troops, which would make it the battle with the greatest number of combatants on British soil.

Edward IV

Towton allowed his coronation as Edward IV and brought the submission of all but the most committed Lancastrians. In order to affirm both his legitimacy and the extent to which his position was not dependent on parliament, Edward emphasised his hereditary right to the Crown, a stance that was to be matched by Richard III and Henry VII.

Edward went on to suppress continued Lancastrian opposition, helped by winning over Louis XI of France, to abandon his rivals in 1463. Scotland followed suit, and in 1464 the Lancastrians in northern England were defeated, with Henry thereafter a fugitive who was eventually captured in 1465. The series, sequence and tempo of Edward's military and political success was impressive.

A headstrong young man used to getting his own way, Edward fell foul of his older cousin, Richard Neville, Earl of Warwick, a key Yorkist, in part due to policy differences and in part as a result of Edward's backing of his wife's relations, the Woodvilles, who challenged Warwick's dominance at Court. Prefiguring Henry VIII's favour for Anne Boleyn, and the problems this created for Cardinal Wolsey, leading to his fall in 1529, the very fact that Edward had secretly married Elizabeth Woodville in 1464 showed that there were limits to Warwick's dominance. He had been negotiating a French marriage for Edward as part of the complex politics of England, France and the latter's rival Burgundy. Marriage was another cause of tension later in the decade when Edward blocked a proposed marriage between George, Duke of Clarence, his younger brother – and, in the absence yet of children, his heir – and Isabel, Warwick's eldest daughter. In 1469, the marriage took place without Edward's permission, being conducted by George, Archbishop of York, Warwick's brother.

Political differences increasingly took a military form. After defeating the royal army at Edgecote on 26 July 1469 and capturing Edward soon after, Warwick seized power. However, he could not maintain his authority and in 1470 he fled to France, Edward regaining power. There Warwick was reconciled with the exiled Queen Margaret of Anjou and committed himself to the restoration of Henry. This was one of the most striking realignments in the opportunistic politics of the period, and one that demonstrated how far power, rather than principle, dominated some aristocratic strategies.

With the help of Louis XI, Warwick and his son-in-law, Clarence, invaded England in 1470. Edward was deposed and forced to flee into exile, and Henry, freed from imprisonment, was restored as king, although he was not mentally in a position to rule.

What Shakespeare, at the close of *Twelfth Night*, termed "the whirligig of time" (V, i), instead brought Edward back again in 1471, benefiting from an alliance with Charles the Bold, Duke of Burgundy, Louis XI's principal opponent. Seizing the initiative, Edward invaded and regained the throne through battle. Moving fast, he defeated and killed Warwick in thick fog at Barnet, north of London. Warwick had been betrayed by Clarence. Edward then defeated the Lancastrians at Tewkesbury, the latter a battle in which he used cannon with success in the early stages. Henry's son, Edward, was murdered after being captured at Tewkesbury: he and other leading Lancastrians were dragged from sanctuary in the abbey. Now, an incubus to Edward IV as there was no danger that Henry's death would leave his son as a more formidable Lancastrian, Henry himself was murdered in the Tower of London, the first king since Richard II in 1400 to be killed. The nature and exact place of his murder are unclear but an exhumation in 1910 revealed damage to Henry's skull.

Edward then ruled with little opposition until he died in 1483, building up his political allies. In contrast to Henry, Edward worked very hard to win the loyalty of London and its leading citizens, on one occasion inviting the Mayor and Aldermen to join him on a hunting party in Waltham Forest. His interest in knighthood was seen in Edward's rebuilding of St George's Chapel, Windsor from 1475. Like earlier monarchs, notably Edward I and Edward III, Edward sought to bolster himself in his subjects' eyes through resort to the cult of chivalry. Edward also spent heavily on Eltham Palace, building a Great Hall.

Nevertheless, there was still Lancastrian sympathy in the country and serious divisions within the ruling house, while France's victory over Burgundy greatly weakened Edward's international position. Clarence had betrayed Warwick and rejoined Edward in 1471, but was sentenced to death in 1478 for treason. He was killed in the Tower of London, drowned in a butt of malmsey wine, according to contemporaries. The Tower had acquired a grisly reputation before the disappearance of Edward V. Edward IV died at forty in 1483, solvent (just) and with England at peace; but too early to leave his twelve-year-old elder son, Edward V, as an adult successor. Edward IV may have died of apoplexy due to his habitual overeating, which he tried to facilitate by means of emetics. Edward had shown excess and self-indulgence in most matters. Pneumonia, malaria and poison are possibilities, but there is no clear account.

EDWARD V

Unlike in 1422, when the far younger Henry VI had been left to grow up as king while a strong regent, his uncle, John, Duke of Bedford, directed affairs, there was a disputed succession in 1483 – which might also have been the consequence had Henry VI died as king to be succeeded by Edward, Prince of Wales. Edward IV's surviving brother, Richard, Duke of Gloucester, fearful of a Woodville takeover and what that might mean for him, but also ambitious, direct and ruthless in a way that Henry VI's uncles had not been, moved swiftly in the last stage of the tension and rivalry between brothers that Shakespeare displays so well. Richard seized power in 1483 on the pretext that Edward IV's marriage to Elizabeth Woodville was invalid and Edward V illegitimate. Those seen as supporters of the twelve-year-old Edward V were mercilessly treated, with William, Lord Hastings and the Woodvilles being killed without trial.

Richard as Protector was acting as king. He sprayed accusations around, including that Elizabeth Woodville had sought to use sorcery against him. Such claims reflected the role of rumour, prophecy and the occult in contemporary culture, and the extent to which they could haunt individuals and be weaponised to haunt society. The anointing of a monarch in a coronation was designed to deal with such threats. Richard had himself crowned before his nephews disappeared. His nephews, Edward and his younger brother, Richard, Duke of York, were declared bastards, on the spurious grounds that Edward IV was already secretly married when he married Elizabeth Woodville, and Richard sent them to the Tower.

Removed from view, the princes swiftly disappeared, and their fate has long been a cause of controversy, with the 'Ricardians', or supporters of Richard's reputation in a longstanding practice, offering ingenious accounts to seek to prove his innocence. However, given Richard's brutal and decisive character, the example of his own and his brother's ruthlessness, particularly in the slaughter of Edward, Prince of Wales, at Tewkesbury in 1471, and the murderous nature of politics in this period, it is likely that the princes were killed. Contemporaries believed that they were dead. Otherwise, it would have been improbable for a rank outsider like Henry Tudor, son of Margaret Beaufort, the heiress of the illegitimate Lancastrian line, to seem a viable figurehead for opposition to Richard. Belief in this murder greatly discredited Richard, a violent man.

RICHARD III

Richard (1483–85) had ability and determination, and inspired the trust of many up to the time of his usurpation in 1483. He had invaded Scotland successfully in 1482, so his military record was good. Moreover, Richard could be pious, as in 1484 when he began preparations for a huge chantry in York to say prayers.

However, Richard's seizure of the throne defied political conventions and divided the Yorkists, and, as a result both of this and of his subsequent treatment of individuals, Richard was left with only a slender base of support. This was shown in October 1483 when the Woodvilles and Henry, 2nd Duke of Buckingham, who himself had played a major role in Richard's seizure of the throne, rebelled. In this crisis, the decisive Richard moved swiftly, dispersing the rebels, most of whom made their peace with Richard or escaped abroad. Buckingham was beheaded at Salisbury.

Christmas at Court, 1484

'During the Christmas feast too much attention was paid to singing and dancing and to vain exchanges of dress between Queen Anne and Lady Elizabeth, eldest daughter of the dead king, who were alike in complexion and figure.'

The Crowland Chronicler

In 1485, another exile, another campaign. Henry Tudor was from the Tudors of Penmynydd, a prominent Welsh family of offi-cials and, earlier, leading servants of the rulers of Gwynedd. Edmund Tudor had married Margaret Beaufort, the heiress of the cadet Lancastrian line. Their son Henry was able to thrust himself to the fore thanks to the death of Henry VI and his only child, Edward.

Invading from France, and with its support including troops, Henry was able to land in Pembrokeshire, build up support in Wales and advance into the centre of England, as Henry IV had done in 1399 and Edward IV in 1471. At the battle of Bosworth, John, 1st Duke of Norfolk, the Earl Marshal and Lord High Steward, led Richard's vanguard and was killed by an arrow, while Richard was abandoned both by the Stanleys – an important family, allied to Henry Tudor through Margaret Beaufort – who had brought their troops to the battlefield, and by Henry Percy, 4th Earl of Northumberland, who commanded his rearguard. This reflected Richard's failure to offer good lordship to his supporters from the North. Henry, meanwhile, benefited from the support of skilled French mercenaries. Nevertheless, Richard's cavalry charge represented a chance for victory that reflected the chaotic and far from inevitable nature of the battle, one represented by Richard's ability to kill many of those who were impersonating Henry in order to reduce the risk to him. In the end, Richard fell with the formidable wounds, recently revealed when his burial place was found under a Leicester car park.

HENRY VII

Even so, Henry VII (1485–1509), who had only gained success due to the betrayal of Richard, had to cope with a subsequent series of Yorkist plots, including a full-scale rebellion in 1487 that was defeated at the battle of Stoke, which was the true end of the Wars of the Roses. The Yorkist army there was ostensibly fighting for 'Edward VI', Edward, Earl of Warwick, son of George, Duke of Clarence and nephew of Edward IV, who, in fact, was impersonated by Lambert Simnel, probably the son of an Oxford tradesman. Another nephew, John, 1st Earl of Lincoln, son of Edward IV's sister Elizabeth, played a key role in the rising. He was killed in the battle, and the captured Simnel was given a menial role in the royal kitchens, which was an expression of Henry's contempt, one designed to convey the strength of his position. However, the battle was hard-fought and larger than Bosworth, and Henry knew from Richard's fate that kings could be overthrown all too easily. If Stoke had been won by Lincoln, a Yorkist bandwagon might have begun to roll, a bandwagon that would have affected the subsequent depiction of the Wars of the Roses by William Shakespeare and others.

This invasion/rebellion proved the last of a sequence that had started with Henry of Lancaster's successful one against Richard II in 1399. Plots and royal anxiety, nevertheless, continued for decades thereafter, being centred in 1495–99 on Perkin Warbeck, another impersonator of alleged royalty, and one enjoying Burgundian support. In 1499, Edward, Earl of Warwick, the son of Clarence, who had been kept in the Tower since 1485, was beheaded for treason after being involved in a plot to escape, bringing to an end the legitimate male line of the House of Plantagenet. The execution was probably due to the need to win Spanish support for a royal marriage for Henry's heir Arthur, so that Katherine of Aragon would not find her position as future Queen endangered, and it was claimed that Katherine felt guilty thereafter. Warbeck, who claimed to be the youngest of the sons of Edward IV, one of the 'Princes in the Tower', was hanged for his role in the same escape attempt. In *State Songs* (1715–16), 'James III', the 'Warming Pan Baby', the Jacobite claimant to the throne, was to be compared to Warbeck as a way to delegitimate him. It was only after 1499 that Henry's reign appeared secure.

Although he succeeded unchallenged, plots and anxiety led, under the restlessly anxious and vindictive Henry VIII, to the killing of the last Plantagenets. There was the execution of those with some possible claim on the throne for example, due to the marriage of Edward IV's sister Elizabeth Plantagenet to John, 2nd Duke of Suffolk. Their son, Edmund, Earl of Suffolk, was executed in 1513 after he had been recognised as king by Louis XII of France. His brother Richard then claimed the throne and served the French, only to die in battle. The marriage of Edward IV's youngest daughter, Katherine, to Sir William Courtenay set up another train of killings. Their child, Henry, Marquess of Exeter (Henry VIII's first cousin and former close friend), was executed for treason in 1538, while Margaret, Countess of Salisbury, the surviving daughter of Clarence and mother of Reginald, Cardinal Pole, followed in 1541. Pole was seen as a key figure in organising Continental opposition to Henry VIII, who sought, without success, to have him kidnapped or assassinated.

Henry VII, however, had strengthened the Tudor claim in 1486 by marrying Elizabeth of York, a daughter of Edward IV and sister of the princes killed in the Tower. Henry thus joined his branch of the House of Lancaster to that of York. This process was symbolised by the replacement of the white rose of York and the red rose of the Beauforts (and maybe of Lancaster) by the Tudor rose which impaled both roses in one. As a sign of Welshness, Henry added the red dragon to the royal arms, while, in 1489, the title Prince of Wales was revived for Henry's first son who was significantly named Arthur, only to predecease him in 1502, probably dying of the sweating sickness, a mysterious infectious disease that had been common from 1485.

There was a focusing of authority and patronage on Henry as king, and an attempt to build up links with 'new men' as part of a process in which the Crown had more direct routes to the locally powerful. Although nobles, such as John, 13th Earl of Oxford, a firm opponent of Edward IV, could be trusted by Henry with considerable local power, a determined attempt was made to limit the private armed forces of nobles, and Henry also placed people under bonds (financial guarantees) for good behaviour. This was also a way for him to raise revenue.

Henry's victory at Bosworth in 1485 is still popularly held to mark the close of the Middle Ages in England and thus the beginning of the modern age. The establishment of Henry and, with him, the Tudor dynasty was, and still is, an appropriate point to take stock. By ending the Wars of the Roses, albeit really at the battle of Stoke in 1487 and not at Bosworth, Henry helped to bring a measure of greater unity to the kingdom. Over the previous decades, civil strife had contributed to, as much as it had stemmed from, a serious crisis, both in law and order and, more generally, in royal governance. In turn, there was a change, so that strong royal authority, as seen under Henry VII and Henry VIII, was an eventual consequence of the earlier collapse of stability in the 1450s, 1460–1, 1469–71, and 1483–85. This authority was challenged and qualified during the following century, including in an unsuccessful Cornish rising in 1497, and notably repeatedly in 1536–69, but it was the basis for the political order that survived.

Just as James IV (1488–1513) restored royal power and prestige in Scotland, and Henry II, Edward I and Edward III earlier had done so in England, so Henry VII was to do the same. Both were effective and hardworking managers of the baronial politics of their realms and also made the business of government, and especially of finances, effective. Indeed, the two British monarchies were in a good stage at the start of the sixteenth century.

Yet, the English one was no longer a cross-Channel presence, although Calais was retained by England until 1558, the claim to the French throne was only abandoned in the reign of George III, and the Channel Isles, the last of the Norman legacy, are still held by the Crown. Nevertheless, France had been effectively lost in 1453. There were to be further invasions of France by Edward IV, Henry VII and Henry VIII, each of whom entertained a wish to regain the lost glory and power of the kings of England in France, as when Henry VII decided in 1489 on new coins that included the royal arms of England and France. Henry VIII mounted very expensive invasions of France, in 1512, 1513, 1522–3, and 1544, that produced short-term territorial gains: Tournai in 1513 and Boulogne in 1544, and, in 1512, there was interest in restoring the processes of pre-1453 government in south-west France. However, the failure of these rulers to achieve their ambitions in France was important to the development of the insular nature of English and, later, British monarchy.

As a result, there is a natural break in the history of monarchy in this period. It may be convenient to see this break essentially with the change of dynasty, and, therefore, with the course and consequences of the Wars of the Roses. That would be mistaken as the changes of note were not simply due to those of monarch, while there was no comparable change in Scotland. Rulers were most obviously prominent as military leaders, and this had even been true for Richard II, who had led expeditions which is not how he tends to be remembered. From that perspective, failure against France was a key context for a troubled kingship, and was clearly felt in that light by successive rulers.

There was, however, little that Henry VI could have done differently in order to avoid this outcome. It was not simply that he was no warrior king like his father, for other factors were also involved. These included the problems of maintaining a position against attack. As John, and also the far more impressive Edward III in his last years, had discovered, this was not an easy task, and was certainly far less prestigious than that of making conquests. Henry VI and his ministers failed at consolidation, but, in addition, Henry was scarcely a monarch for the decisive climax of the Hundred Years' War in the early 1450s. He took no direct role in trying to reverse the rapid French gains then, but, far from being 'sounds off', they were to help remove the vital lubricant of stability provided by success, both the reality of achievement, and the sense of a monarch who was the master of affairs. Henry VI lacked both characteristics.

Henry VII was buried in the Henry VII Lady Chapel at the east end of Westminster Abbey, one of the glories of English Perpendicular architecture, which was built during his reign. The tomb, by the Florentine artist Pietro Torrigiano, was one of the very first examples of Italian Renaissance design to be introduced into Britain. So also, in replacement of the burning down of Sheen Palace the previous year, with the building from 1498 of Richmond Palace which had Renaissance features. In these steps, as in so much else, Henry's reign represented a transition.

3

Sixteenth-Century Developments

....

With Henry VIII (1509–47) and Elizabeth I (1558–1603) presiding, the Tudors tend to come first when discussing British monarchy in the sixteenth century. Henry's six wives and the Spanish Armada of 1588 provide drama enough, but on top of those comes 'Bloody Mary' (1553–8) and mid-century crisis. And yet, drama is even more pronounced in Scotland. It is there that one monarch, James IV, was killed and another, Mary, Queen of Scots, was defeated and fled. Civil conflict and foreign war are both more disruptive in Scotland than in England and we shall begin there.

SCOTLAND

Under James IV (1488–1513) and his infant successor James V (1513–42), the authority of the Scottish monarchy increased, but war abroad brought disaster. Whereas England was separated by the English Channel and its increasing naval strength from more populous and powerful Continental neighbours, there was no such defence from England for Scotland. Instead, Scotland looked to France as England's leading opponent, although in doing so, the kings of Scotland helped cement English enmity and ensure that it was acted upon.

There is a tendency to see the late fifteenth century as some sort of transition to modernity and not least in terms of the Renaissance, printing and, more mundanely, 'new monarchies' better able to execute policies as was soon to be seen with the Protestant Reformation. Yet, there was also continuity. In 1346,

David II invaded England, only to be defeated at Neville's Cross and imprisoned in England until 1357. In 1513, James IV invaded, but was totally defeated and killed at Flodden. Similarly, in 1488, James III was defeated by aristocratic rebels at Sauchieburn and killed soon after. In 1568, his great-granddaughter, Mary, Queen of Scots, was overthrown, forced to abdicate, defeated at Langdale, and fled to England, never to return. This theme of continuity also underlined the chance factors, notably of warfare, that helped ensure the folly of drawing patterns in the eddies of time; this is true both for contemporaries drawing these patterns and for our doing so.

As a reminder of the values of the period, there was a religious reckoning for Flodden, part of an honouring of victory. James IV's banner, sword and thigh-armour were taken to the shrine of St Cuthbert in Durham Cathedral, while the gold crucifix worn by James, including a fragment of the True Cross, was taken for Henry VIII and placed in the Tower of London. The fragment made this crucifix of great totemic significance.

James IV had invaded England in 1513, in part because of the outbreak of war between the latter and France. Henry VIII was in France, waging a campaign without real consequence, when a smaller army under Thomas, Earl of Surrey, later 3rd Duke of Norfolk, outfought and heavily defeated the invading Scots. This, however, did not lead to any English intervention in Scotland. Instead, James V was able to benefit from peace with Henry. Initially, his mother, Margaret Tudor, a sister of Henry VIII, was Guardian, while a General Council of the Realm reached for power. Margaret married Archibald Douglas, 6th Earl of Angus, in 1514, and this led other nobles opposed to him to turn to John, Duke of Albany, a grandson of James II, the heir-presumptive, and a pro-French figure. Margaret lost her position, only to replace Albany in a coup in 1524 while he was in France. Margaret was formally recognised as the Chief Councillor to James, only for Angus, from whom Margaret was separated, to seize power in

1525. Two years later, Pope Clement VII granted her petition for a divorce, an outcome her brother Henry was not to obtain. In 1528, James gained power and Angus fled. Margaret regained influence, but James became increasingly independent of his mother, not least of her wish for better relations between him and Henry.

James, meanwhile, crushed aristocratic opposition as he established his power with expeditions to the Borders in 1530 and to the Western Isles in 1540, a frequent task for his predecessors. Like Henry, but more so, James also resisted Protestantism. He sought, in the Parliament of 1541, to protect Catholicism but favoured a measure of reform and gained greater power over the Church. Alliance with France, however, led to English invasion in 1542. Defeat at Solway Moss was followed soon after by James's death, and the succession was left to his new-born daughter, Mary, Queen of Scots, his daughter by Mary of Guise, a member of the mighty French Guise family. Scotland appeared to have the choice of English or French control, as both intervened with more energy from 1547.

Meanwhile, Wales had been absorbed into the English parliamentary and legal system in 1536–43, while the developing Reformation Crisis led to a new situation in Ireland. In 1534, Thomas, Earl of Kildare, rebelled, offering the overlordship of Ireland to the Pope or the Emperor Charles V, in place of the schismatic Henry. Victory for the latter in 1535 was followed by Henry gaining more power and authority, with Parliament exalting him, first as the 'Supreme Head' of the Irish Church and then, in 1541, as 'King of Ireland', rather than its Lord.

HENRY VIII

The transformation of monarchy in the British Isles owed much to Henry (1509–47), and it is to him that we should turn. Seeing himself as a warrior king, one in the tradition of past heroes, notably Edward III and Henry V, Henry loved (and lived when he could) the display and machismo of royal warfare and campaigned in person against the French in 1513, 1523 and 1544, winning the (minor) battle of the Spurs in 1513. No later kings were to win successes, other than William III in the 1690s, notably the capture of Namur in 1695, and George II at Dettingen in 1743. Henry's expensive wars led to a violent popular response in 1525 when taxes were raised in what became the far-from-welcome 'Amicable Grant'. Henry also loved competitiveness in other forms, as when he met Francis I of France at the Field of Cloth of Gold in 1520. His zest for grandeur was also seen in his extensive building or rebuilding of palaces, which included work at Bridewell, Eltham, Greenwich, Hampton Court, St James's, Nonsuch, Outlands, Richmond, Thornbury, Westminster, Windsor and Woking. Progresses, pageants, ceremonial entries and tournaments were all part of Henry's zeal to stage monarchy as triumphant and what he saw as truly regal. Display had to be to the fore.

Henry avoided military disaster such as that which led to the death of James IV at Flodden in 1513 or which affected Francis I, who was totally defeated and captured by the Emperor Charles V at Pavia in 1525. Instead, Henry's problem was that of the succession. His wife, Katherine of Aragon, Charles's aunt, bore him five children, but only a daughter, Mary, survived. Unlike in France, rule by a woman was legal in England, but there was concern about the precedent set by the failure of Henry I's daughter, Matilda. Henry convinced himself that his failure to have a son was divine punishment because he had married the widow of his elder brother, Arthur. The marriage in 1509 had been permitted by Pope Julius II, despite the 1501 marriage of Arthur and Katherine; but Henry became increasingly mindful of the Biblical injunction that a man should not have sexual relations with his brother's wife.

Henry was trying to end his marriage before he fell in love with Anne Boleyn. Her refusal to become Henry's mistress, however, came to play a role, as this led Henry to decide that he wanted to marry her, which pressed forward his quest for an annulment. The failure of negotiations resulted in the disgrace in 1529 of Thomas, Cardinal Wolsey, the principal minister, a step reflecting Henry's priorities and anger. However, Wolsey was not executed – or rather, died before he could be.

In 1531, in reaction against the failure of the negotiations and, therefore, against papal legal jurisdiction as a whole, Henry became more forceful in asserting English independence from the Church. He was impressed by the argument that kings possessed imperial authority by divine gift, so that the ruler should not submit to the power of the Church. As a result, he believed papal sanction was not required for the annulment. Henry's views were taken forward with parliamentary support in 1532, as, on a longstanding pattern, the House of Commons was antagonistic to Church officers abusing their power which they sought to restrict.

Henry finally publicly rejected papal jurisdiction in 1533. That year, he also secretly married Anne, and Anne gave birth to the future Elizabeth I. The marriage with Katherine was annulled by the new Archbishop of Canterbury, Thomas Cranmer, whom Shakespeare presents as defended from false accusations by Henry, which indeed happened. The annulment made valid the marriage with Anne, a Catholic (like Henry) who sympathised with some aspects of Protestantism. Princess Mary now became illegitimate. The Act of Succession of that year bastardised Mary and therefore placed the children of his marriage to Anne first in the succession, which so far meant Elizabeth. The problem of a female successor had not been ended, only complicated.

This emphasis in England on policy and its defence led to the expression of what was, by the standards of the age, nationalism. This nationalism focused not only on present politics, lay and ecclesiastical, but also on an account of the past, while the politics, in turn, encouraged a fresh interpretation of English history.

In the preamble to the Act in Restraint of Appeals [to Rome] of 1533, an Act that proclaimed jurisdictional self-sufficiency and rejected appeals to Rome, it was claimed, in The Tudor Constitution, that 'by divers sundry old authentic histories and chronicles, it is manifestly declared and expressed that this realm of England is an empire, and so hath been accepted in the world, governed by one supreme head and king, having the dignity and royal estate of the imperial crown of the same'. This assertion by Henry looked back to the house of Wessex's claims of overlordship in Britain in the tenth and eleventh centuries, an overlordship rooted in control of England but not restricted to it. Indeed, Wales was to be absorbed under Henry into the English parliamentary and legal system, while the authority of the Common Law, a national law, was pushed to the fore. Tudor monarchs now wore the arched crowns of imperial authority.

The past was a continuing presence for Henry, who was no Protestant, and did not wish to see any abandonment of the Catholic faith – as was shown, after the break with Rome, by the attack on heresy, i.e. Protestantism, with the Act of Six Articles in 1539. However, in accordance with a providential grasp of kingship, and therefore himself, Henry had a 'conversion' to his new ecclesiastical position. He resolved to take charge of the Church and came to see himself as like the kings of Israel in the Old Testament. The Book of Kings in the Old Testament of the Bible was that most frequently used for readings. In 1536, royal injunctions specified the doctrines to be taught in church. Henry formulated a distinctive type of Christianity while claiming to free the English Church from the evil of papal usurpation and corrupt practices. As far as the latter were concerned, the rejection of miracles and relics was a major change.

By the Act of Supremacy of 1534, Henry became the 'Supreme Head' of the Church of England. The impact of Henry's policies was therefore to make the ecclesiastical situation in England dependent on English politics. The Treason Act made it treasonable to deny this supremacy. Conformity in belief, rather than just act, was now required. Under this statute, prominent critics such as Thomas More, the former Chancellor, and John Fisher, Bishop of Rochester, were executed, in 1535.

Anne's failure to produce a son endangered her position. She succumbed to factional hostility motivated by concern about her allies and policies. The conservatives at court were joined in this case by Thomas Cromwell, Henry's key minister and a onetime protégé of Wolsey. Tried on the probably trumped-up charge of adultery in 1536, Anne was beheaded. John Wesley, the eighteenth-century Methodist leader, was to refer to Henry as making 'the law the engine of his boisterous passions'. As Anne's marriage was now declared void, Elizabeth was bastardised. Henry then married the innocuous Jane Seymour. She produced his only legitimate son to survive, Edward, in 1537; Jane died soon after.

The birth of Edward ensured that Henry had a male succession to protect, and this helped close the path to any return to a more Catholic option, because that would have focused on Mary. Treason was extended to words, not just deeds, which was a major extension of the legal position of the monarch. The dissolution of the monasteries in 1536–40 changed life in many localities and was a potent demonstration of Henry's will and power. The counterpoint was the palaces he built for himself, notably one that was aptly called Nonsuch. The attack on saints' cults was another breach with the past.

Meanwhile, although Henry's stance at Court and in the favouritism of power might be unpredictable, he was consistent in directing royal authority and in creating fear of its use. The law was manipulated by a suspicious and insecure, indeed paranoid, king ready to use deceit and violence to overcome the reality of problems. When he came to the throne, the shrewd Henry showed a ruthless opportunism in executing two of his father's unpopular ministers, Sir Richard Empson and Edmund Dudley. As a reminder of the extent to which individuals and families recur in different settings, Dudley's son, John, Duke of Northumberland, was executed in 1553 for being the force behind the unsuccessful coup on behalf of Lady Jane Grey, while the younger son of Northumberland, Robert, Earl of Leicester, was a favourite of Elizabeth I. Leicester's stepson, Robert, 2nd Earl of Essex, led the failed coup against Elizabeth's ministers in 1601 and was beheaded, and the son of the latter, Robert, 3rd Earl of Essex, was the first Captain-General of the Parliamentary army against Charles I in the English Civil War. Execution was the fate of many who hugged close to Henry, but also of those who defied his policies, whether elderly clerics or provincials demonstrating their unhappiness. Meanwhile, heretics, such as Anne Askew in 1546, continued to be burnt to death.

Marital change was linked to ministerial fortune. Henry found his fourth wife, Anne of Cleves, the sister of a reforming Catholic German prince whose policies might have seemed close to Henry's, unappealing, and he swiftly rejected her. This rejection was linked to the fall and execution of the meritocratic chief minister, Thomas Cromwell, whose promotion to the Earldom of Essex could not free him from unpopularity in the eyes of much of the aristocracy. Henry had turned to marital youth in the form of Katherine Howard, a member of the conservative Howard faction, and the conservative faction exploited Cromwell's unwillingness to support Henry's favour for her. Cromwell was executed on the day of the marriage. Katherine, however, proved another short-lived Queen, and she was executed for adultery in 1542. She had certainly recklessly shown favour to young courtiers, and adultery on the part of a queen left no room for compromise. As with Anne Boleyn and, later, Lady Jane Grey and Mary, Queen of Scots, Katherine was given the relative dignity of beheading, rather than hanging.

His last wife, Katherine Parr, a widow who was sympathetic to Protestantism, proved able to manage him – or at least survive; although only after seeing off a major challenge to her position based on hostility to her evangelical activities. In contrast, the Howards were disgraced at the end of the reign: Henry, Earl of Surrey, was executed on a charge of treasonably quartering the royal arms (bringing them into his coat of arms symbol for his family); while his disgraced father, Thomas, 3rd Duke of Norfolk, who had served Henry with great energy, survived only because Henry died the day before that appointed for his execution.

These moves led to the overshadowing of the more conservative faction at court, that which was closest to Catholicism. Power was left to Edward's uncle, Jane Seymour's brother, Edward, Earl of Hertford, who became Protector and Duke of Somerset.

Henry changed English kingship by making it more central to the religious position and life of the country, a situation that was to cause fundamental problems for the Stuarts. Anticipating the seventeenth-century issue of whether a ruler's religion had to be adopted by his subjects, he had no doubts on the matter. Indeed, in the frontispiece of the Great Bible, copies of which were to be placed in every parish church, a true reach for government, Henry was presented as a prophet, bringing the Biblical words of God in English to his bishops who take it on to a people who shout out 'Vivat rex'.

In Henry, a new dynasty also created a new aristocracy, such as the Russells, later Dukes of Bedford, a dukedom based in large part on former Church lands, largely released by the dissolution of the monasteries. The future relationship between this group and the Crown, however, was also to be very unsettled. In part, this was because the Crown, as ever, was an abstraction that covered the very different attitudes and circumstances of individual monarchs. This was particularly so in the case of Henry's successors as, with his three children by different marriages, and his changes in ecclesiastical policy and foreign alignments, he had fractured any sense of Tudor continuity. Monarchs, like later Prime Ministers, have to a degree to be judged by what came after, because it is what they establish and leave that is crucial, even though it is understandably difficult to control, or even influence, the route taken by successors.

Determined, energetic and hardworking, Henry had kept his grip on the domestic situation, helped by his clear right to the throne, his unwillingness to turn too obviously to either religious option, and the selective use of terror, for example the execution of the Duke of Buckingham in 1521 and the Marquess of Exeter in 1538. He retained control of the government, as well as of the aristocracy through their attendance at court, through the court itself travelling, through shared participation in military activities and the hunt, and through patronage. These were more important than institutional state-building, for, although there were changes in government practices, Henry's preference for direct control remained the key theme.

EDWARD VI

The situation was less favourable under Henry's successors, for the next four, respectively, were an infant (Edward VI, 1547–53), a woman (Mary, 1553–8), a woman (Elizabeth I, 1558–1603), and a foreigner (James I, 1603–25). Each of these posed problems. In one light, the fact that each survived, to die in their beds, was a sign of the strength of monarchy, and the degree to which Henry VII and Henry VIII, who also died in their beds, had lain firm foundations. There was no recurrence of the Wars of the Roses, and, notably, of Richard III's coup in 1483. All bar Mary succeeded unchallenged. Yet, looked at differently, there was a sustained mid-sixteenth century crisis, from the risings in Lincolnshire and Yorkshire in 1536 to those in the far North in 1569, and these were simply the most obvious manifestation of a situation surmounted by chance, violence, and guile. A punctuated civil war was in some respects akin to the civil war of the Wars of the Roses, but, due to the religious dimension, that under the Tudors was more serious.

Like those of Henry III, Richard II and Henry VI, the last minority, that of Edward V in 1483, did not augur well. Somerset sought power but was not a sinister figure as had been Richard, Duke of Gloucester, later Richard III. Instead, Somerset's focus was on the consolidation of Protestantism. Edward is generally seen as an enthusiastic Protestant. Wesley wrote of Edward, 'Such a prodigy of understanding and virtue was taken unsullied to the GOD whom he loved.' The extent of Edward's Protestantism, however, has been disputed, and, separately, it has been argued that the drive to Protestantism came primarily from his ministers. This drive helped provoke a major rebellion in the South-West in 1549, the Prayer-Book Rebellion. That was brutally suppressed, as was that in Norfolk focused on opposition to agrarian change.

The Homily on Obedience, 1547

'The high power and authority of kings, with their making of laws, judgments and officers, are the ordinances not of man but of God . . . We may not resist nor in any wise hurt, an anointed king which is God's lieutenant, vicegerent and highest minister in that country where he is king.'

Drawn up under the guidance of Thomas Cranmer, Archbishop of Canterbury and issued under the authority of Edward VI, this homily was to be read out in church four times a year.

There was already tension within the government, including over the royal family. In early 1549, Somerset's ambitious and volatile younger brother, Sir Thomas Seymour, who, having married Henry's widow Katherine Parr, had tried to seduce Elizabeth when she was thirteen, was arrested and executed for plotting to gain power by seizing Edward and marrying Elizabeth, prefiguring the gamble seen with Robert, 2nd Earl of Essex, in 1601. Seymour had sought recognition as Governor of Edward's person. In turn, the provincial risings destabilised Somerset's government and led to his being overthrown by aristocratic opponents on the Council in 1549 and beheaded three years later. Edward played no real role in this change, which was one among the many that had begun with the overthrow of Cardinal Wolsey in 1529.

The crucial new figure was John Dudley, Earl of Warwick, who became Lord President of the Council in 1550–3, and Duke of Northumberland in 1551. An experienced soldier and member of Henry's service nobility, he was more committed than many to pushing through a clearcut Protestantism.

As so often, uncertainty over the royal succession came athwart plans, but this was made more serious by the religious complexion of politics. In 1551, a mission to France to try to arrange a marriage between Edward and Elizabeth, daughter of Henry II of France, did not take place. Northumberland's position was endangered by Edward's poor health, which led the duke to persuade the unmarried Edward to exclude his half-sisters, Mary and Elizabeth, from the succession. Instead, Lady Jane Grey, granddaughter of Henry VII through his second daughter, a weak claim, was declared next in line in Edward's will. She was married to Guildford Dudley, one of Northumberland's sons, a very clear demonstration of ambition, and when Edward died in July 1553, probably of respiratory disease, which was particularly deadly in the period, she was proclaimed queen.

MARY

There was no inherent reason why this coup should have failed. Jane was a woman, but so was the rival claimant, Henry's daughter Mary. Jane was a Protestant, but Catholicism had been weakened over the previous two decades. In practice, as with Henry VII's success in 1485, there were people willing to fight for Jane, but many reluctant to commit themselves to risk. Also, as with 1485, chance in the shape of the interaction of events and determination proved crucial. In marked contrast to Edward V and Gloucester in 1483, Northumberland had not secured control of Mary, who, showing her father's determination, proclaimed herself queen in Norwich and began raising troops among the local aristocracy and gentry. Northumberland set out from London to defeat her, but his support crumbled away. The county elites, London, and the Council all rallied to Mary, who seems to have gained popular support. Without a battle, Northumberland abandoned his effort and was arrested. Lady Jane's reign had lasted nine days, and soon after the failed queen-maker was executed.

A convinced and brave Catholic born in 1516, Mary (1553–8), unlike her predecessor Edward, and would-be replacement Jane, was of an age and determination to make her own decisions. Determined to undo the Reformation, and helped by Northumberland's total failure, she pushed through the repeal of the English Reformation with the exception of the confiscation of former Church lands. Mary appreciated the need to avoid alienating the many powerful who had benefited from this confiscation.

To secure a Catholic succession, Mary determined to marry her younger first cousin, Philip of Spain, the only son of Charles V. In truth, there were very few princes available at her rank, a problem that was to affect her successor Elizabeth, but with Mary being further restricted because she would only consider marrying a co-religionist. The marriage plan resulted in a rebellion in Kent led by Sir Thomas Wyatt. Initially a threat, it was defeated, in large part due to leading nobles standing firm. Mary, who again responded to crisis bravely, publicly gave an effective speech at London's Guildhall, then displayed her father's firmness in disposing of potential rivals. Jane Grey, her husband and her father, were all executed. Her fate was to be seen as tragic. Nicholas Rowe's play *Lady Jane Grey* (1715) became a Whig classic.

Rowe was made Poet Laureate by George I, while, as children, the future George III and his siblings staged this account of exemplary Protestant constancy and pathos.

Mary's half-sister Elizabeth had been implicated in the plot, but Mary preferred to detain her. Having married Philip, Mary pressed on with re-Catholicisation while also restoring older aristocratic families against whom Henry had turned. The reaction against the Reformation saw Mary discard the phrase 'of blessed memory' when making reference to Henry.

Mary's reign was one of the great might-have-beens of English royal history, but this was cut short in two respects. First, Mary did not have her hoped-for heir. Second, she was sickly and died from influenza in 1558. There had been plans to exclude Elizabeth and have Philip crowned, but they were not brought to fruition. Mary's reign ended up as a counterpoint against which that of Elizabeth was to be judged. Mary and Elizabeth are buried together in the Lady Chapel in Westminster Abbey, with Mary, Queen of Scots across the nave from them, all a type of posthumous royal reconciliation in which birth trumps all.

Mary Recalled

Mary's image was softened in the *Ecclesiastical History of Great Britain* (1708–14) by the High Church Tory Jeremy Collier, whereas the anti-Catholic Gilbert Burnet's *History of the Reformation* (1715) saw Providence at work in Mary's foreshortened reign, with Elizabeth, in turn, seen as a model of a good monarch who 'looked on her people as her children'.

The popularity of Mary's policy of re-Catholicisation and the attempt to rehabilitate her reputation are matters of debate for scholars. So is the question of what would have happened if her reign had lasted for longer. Would Mary have gone on reigning against the background of the burning of Protestants begun in February 1555? By the time she died, the Protestant leaders in England had been killed. This had deprived Protestantism of both leadership and cohesion, as well as challenging its morale and hopes for the future. That the burnings persisted into 1558 reveals that Protestantism continued to have supporters but also the determination and ability to sustain repression. More than outward conformity to restored Catholicism had been achieved.

Large-scale repression was to work in Austria, Bohemia and France, all of which experienced forcible and successful re-Catholicisation over the following 150 years. There was no time for this in England, and Mary was the last monarch to give out 'cramp rings' to ward off leprosy, an example of a legitimising practice dating back to Edward the Confessor.

Yet, the prospect of a different outcome suggests how Mary's reputation could have been very different, a situation that would have put the reputation of Edward VI in a different light. Moreover, Philip II had children by his next marriage, which underlines the contingencies surrounding Mary's reign. In the event, she was to be 'Bloody Mary', the cause of a Protestant martyrology that was effectively disseminated in *Acts and Monuments of the Church* (1563) by John Foxe, popularly known as the *Book of Martyrs*. After an order of 1571, cathedral churches acquired copies, and many parish churches chose to do likewise. Other works on the reign included the 1600s play *The Famous History of Sir Thomas Wyatt* by Thomas Dekker and John Webster.

MARY, QUEEN OF SCOTS

In dealing with religious and other issues, the role of unpredictability was to be readily seen in comparing Elizabeth, who came to the throne in 1558, with Mary, Queen of Scots. Although the latter was younger, she had no elder siblings and her father, James

V, died in 1542. French influence in Scotland increased with Mary sent to France in 1548, and in 1558 she was married to Francis, the heir to the French throne, a marriage that served the French geopolitical goal of fixing Scotland in enmity to England. He became Francis II the following year, when his father, Henry II, died unexpectedly as a result of a joust at a tournament.

Mary's personal and geopolitical future was thus opposed to that of Mary of England, and, indeed, in 1558, French forces had captured Calais from an England then, as an ally of Philip II, at war with France. A Franco-Scottish monarchy appeared in prospect, a personal union that would possibly have been similar to that between England and Scotland from 1603 to 1707. Moreover, such a union might well have challenged both the English position in Ireland and that of the Tudors in England. There was no sense that the histories of the dynasties or their territories were separate.

This prospect of a Franco-Scottish monarchy ended in 1560. Francis II died leaving Mary a childless widow. The next two French kings, brothers of Francis II, were also to lack children, as was the brother who did not become king, and the Valois dynasty came to an end in 1589, although without the consequence for Anglo-French relations of the end of the Capetian dynasty in 1328. The failure of this union, like that of Philip II and Mary Tudor, to produce either a child or an alliance that survived the marriage serves as a reminder that diplomacy helped make major developments possible but could only achieve so much. Mary had no consequence now in French politics, in contrast to her mother-in-law, Catherine de Medici, who had royal sons on the throne from 1559 to 1589, as later, in the shape of Louis XIII (1610–43), did Marie de Medici, the widow of Henry IV, the first of the Bourbon dynasty.

Mary, in contrast, had a kingdom of her own. She returned to Scotland in 1561, but the previous year, her mother, Mary of Guise, the widow of James V, had been deposed as Regent by the Lords of the Congregation, Protestant nobles. With English military, particularly naval, help in 1560, they secured the expulsion of the French garrisons, while the Edinburgh Parliament pushed through Protestantism in Scotland. When Mary, Queen of Scots, formally entered Edinburgh in 1561, she was confronted by Protestant symbols.

Less cautious than Elizabeth in England, but also operating in a more difficult political situation, not least in the aftermath of civil war, Mary did not ratify these changes. Yet, she lacked the political ability to reverse them or to build up a strong body of support in the complex and bitter world of Scottish baronial factionalism. The Lords of the Congregation and their successors united against a Catholic monarch and the French alliance.

Moreover, Mary's marital problems increased her unpopularity. Her second marriage, to her cousin, Lord Darnley, the grandson of Henry VIII's elder sister Margaret by her second husband, in 1565, was unsuccessful; and in 1566 he played a role in the murder of her favourite, David Rizzio. Mary possibly then conspired with the brutal James, Earl of Bothwell, who murdered Darnley and married her in 1567. This was an unpopular step and, in 1567, Mary was forced to surrender to the Protestant Lords and to abdicate in favour of the infant James VI, her son by Darnley, and the third Scottish monarch in succession to come to the throne as a child.

Prefiguring the failure in the 1590s of Sigismund III Vasa, King of Poland, to also retain his throne in Sweden, a Catholic monarch had been overthrown in what was becoming a Protestant realm. In part, circumstances were very different to England when first Northumberland and then Wyatt unsuccessfully challenged Mary Tudor in 1552 and 1554 respectively. Mary, Queen of Scots' enforced abdication in 1567 also prefigured the failure of James VII (of Scotland) and II (of England) to retain power in 1688-9.

James VI

Mary escaped in 1568, only to be defeated at Langside and flee to England to the mercy of Elizabeth. The abdication of Mary encouraged the expression of ideas about the responsibility of the Crown to the people that qualified any authoritarian stress on the duties owed by subjects. This contractual theory of kingship was pushed by the leaders of the Church, not least George Buchanan who became tutor of James VI (1567–1625). One of the longest-lasting of monarchs, he tends to be discussed by English historians as James I (1603–25), and as part of a declining trajectory of competence from Elizabeth I to Charles I.

But, looked at differently, James VI was far more successful than Mary, as indeed he had to be were he to survive. He struggled as a young man to avoid the dominance of an aristocratic Presbyterian faction, but, as he grew to adulthood, gradually acquired an ability to manoeuvre and, with that, greater confidence. Assuming power in 1585, he still faced opposition from the Presbyterian General Assembly, notably in 1596. From a difficult background, he became a skilful monarch. As a result of dynastic chance, James was to be called upon to play his hand in a difficult setting. He did so due to the chances of a monarch who lived for nearly as long as him.

Elizabeth I

Queen for forty-four years, Elizabeth I (1558–1603) was the longest-reigning English monarch since Edward III (1327–77), and her longevity and personality played a major role in determining the political and religious character of Tudor England. Born in 1533, Elizabeth was the longest-living English monarch and was not to be surpassed until George II. As with the accession of Marys in England and Scotland, she came to the throne owing to her legitimate succession and the lack of viable alternatives, and not because stronger central monarchies were less beholden to aristocratic dislike of female rulers. Avoiding marriage and the perils of child-birth were clearly helpful, but Elizabeth's longevity was still remark-able; although in Scotland, William the Lion lived from 1143 until 1214 and Robert II from 1316 until 1390. In contrast, had Elizabeth lived only as long as her half-brother, Edward VI, she would never have become queen, while, if she had matched her half-sister, Mary, or her grandfather Henry VII, she would have died before Mary, Queen of Scots; unless Elizabeth had had Mary executed earlier than 1587. Through the marriage of her grandfather, James IV, to Henry VII's daughter Margaret in 1503, Mary had a good claim to the succession, if Elizabeth remained unmarried, or married and childless. Elizabeth nearly died of smallpox in 1563 and there were a series of later plans to assassinate her.

Elizabeth's longevity, determination, caution and political adeptness played a major role in restoring a measure of political stability after the confusion of mid-century, a restoration which was important both for the succession and for the religious settle-ment. In the latter, Elizabeth had benefited from a humanist education, from an upbringing in which she had been obliged to accommodate two different regimes, and from reversals of fortune. Unlike Edward and Mary, she lacked a personal religious zeal and a commitment to a particular outcome. Instead, caution encouraged Elizabeth to establish a single national Church designed to incorporate people of different views. While doctri-nally Protestant, Elizabeth compromised on what she saw as 'externals'. Her choice to be termed Supreme Governor of the Church of England, more modest than Supreme Head, may have reflected her position as a woman, but was to be continued by all her successors. She did not try to look into men's consciences. Outward conformity was all she sought. Determined to keep royal control over the Church, its bishops, doctrine and liturgy, Elizabeth faced opposition both from Catholics and from more radical Protestants, or Puritans.

Under Mary, Elizabeth had conformed and attended Mass by necessity. When she came to the throne, Elizabeth dismissed most of Mary's ministers and favourites, but, far from being able to fix on a clearly moderate solution, the domestic political situation led Elizabeth in a more Protestant direction. At Christmas 1558, Elizabeth walked out of the Mass when Owen Oglethorpe, Bishop of Carlisle, the only bishop who had been prepared to crown her, elevated the host, a Catholic step, after she had told him not to do so. The following May, he and the other bishops who refused to take the Oath of Supremacy were deprived.

Religious issues were also important in international links. Negotiations in the 1560s for a marriage between Elizabeth and the Austrian Habsburg archduke Charles, brother to the Emperor Maximilian II and cousin of Philip II, failed in part because of an unwillingness to grant the Catholic Charles the right to a private Mass in the royal household. These and other negotiations provide evidence of the able and well-educated Elizabeth's skill in other languages, notably French and Italian.

Attempts to persuade Elizabeth to marry and secure the succession were made by her ministers, and some were staged, for example in *Gorboduc* (1561), a play by Thomas Norton and Thomas Sackville performed before Elizabeth in the Inner Temple in 1562, and also in the entertainment she received from Thomas, 3rd Earl of Sussex, when staying at his country seat in 1579. These marriage schemes all failed, and the Catholicism of the key suitors was a major reason for this failure. In contrast, there was support for a Protestant marriage, notably with Robert Dudley, Earl of Leicester (1532–88), the third son of the Duke of Northumberland executed in 1553, who had himself been condemned to death under Mary in 1554, only to be released. There was a romantic relationship between Elizabeth and Leicester for a while, one that Elizabeth clearly enjoyed, but there is no evidence of a sexual one. Leicester's first wife, Amy Robsart, died in 1560 from a mysterious fall down a flight of stairs, which left him free to remarry, but did not improve his reputation.

In dealing with these and other issues, Elizabeth became the most experienced politician in her kingdom, an experience also sustained by her knowledge of the country stemming from twenty-three summer progresses. Keen on maintaining the royal prerogative, Elizabeth generally knew when to yield, and was usually dexterous in making concessions without appearing weak. A skilled manipulator of courtiers, Elizabeth was able to get the best out of her ministers. She had favourites, but was prepared to sacrifice them for political advantage. Elizabeth used the personal tensions and factional rifts between her ministers and courtiers in order to retain freedom of manoeuvre, a process eased by the extent to which the Protestant interest was divided. Thus, in seeking to constrain the support for Puritanism by Leicester and his elder brother, Ambrose, 3rd Earl of Warwick, Elizabeth could turn to other Protestants, notably Sussex, Lord Chamberlain from 1572 to 1583, and Sir Christopher Hatton. Reasonably successful in coping with divisions among her advisors, Elizabeth, however, found it difficult to control her military commanders. As a different problem, she was intelligent and generally pragmatic, but found it hard to adjust to change.

Elizabeth was affected by stereotypical views of women, not least the assumption that she should marry. She did not condemn the established male view of women as inferior to men. Instead, Elizabeth claimed that she was an exceptional woman because chosen by God as his instrument.

Ironically, although her foremost opponent was to be a man, Philip II of Spain, her leading rival was a woman, Mary, Queen of Scots, whose presence from 1568 acted as a focus of discontent. Indeed, in 1569, there was a conspiracy at Court to replace Elizabeth's leading minister, William Cecil, and to marry Thomas, 4th Duke of Norfolk, a leading religious conservative and son of the Earl of Surrey executed in 1547, to Mary, Queen of Scots, and acknowledge her as heir to the throne. This conspiracy was thwarted at Court, but triggered a rising in the North by its supporters, particularly the Earls of Northumberland and Westmorland, whose local positions were endangered by a lack of royal favour.

The Northern Rising was followed by the Pope excommunicating and deposing Elizabeth, which had not happened to Henry VIII. A number of conspiracies sought to give effect to this on behalf of Mary, especially the Ridolfi (1572), Throckmorton (1582) and Babington (1586) plots. Encouraged by the Papal Bull, the Ridolfi Plot proposed a papal-backed invasion of England by the Duke of Alba, commander of the Spanish army in the Low Countries, in order to help Mary, who was fully involved – as was the Spanish ambassador. Norfolk was executed in 1572 for his role in the plot. The Throckmorton Plot was a response to the failure of marriage negotiations between Elizabeth and Francis, Duke of Anjou, brother to Henry III of France. In 1581, the twenty-six-year-old Anjou came in person to pursue his attempt on the hand of Elizabeth, then forty-seven. She publicly announced the match before rapidly changing her mind. The involvement of successive Spanish envoys in conspiracies compromised relations, while Spain was also aligned with the Catholic League in France, whose leaders, the Guise family, were ardent supporters of their niece, Mary.

Elizabeth was reluctant to try Mary, a fellow sovereign and a relative, but, in 1586, the interception of Mary's correspondence indicated that she had agreed to Elizabeth's assassination. As a result, Mary was convicted of treason. This was a questionable charge as she owed Elizabeth no allegiance. Mary was beheaded at Fotheringay Castle in 1587. Elizabeth was angry with her ministers about the execution, to which she felt she had been driven by pressure as well as necessity. 'The cruel usurper Elizabeth Tudor' was how two pupils referred to her when showing me around the Jesuit boarding school Stonyhurst in the mid-1980s. Hating feeling constrained, Elizabeth was unwilling to confirm James's position in the succession, but granted him an annual payment.

Conflict within the family of related monarchs saw Elizabeth go to war with her former half-brother-in-law, Philip II, in 1585. Spanish invasion in the shape of the Armada was defeated in 1588, and her resolve, notably her speech at Tilbury, was to cast Elizabeth for posterity in a heroic light. However, the difficulties of the war, which continued until 1604, combined with financial problems, divisions over Puritanism, and social strains, and helped give Elizabeth's last years a very difficult and bitter tinge. Parliamentary opposition became more prominent. Henry VIII's use of Parliament to legitimate his dynastic and constitutional objectives had increased its frequency and role, and, despite his wishes, and largely due to the minority of Edward VI, parliamentary management became a more important task for the government.

Elizabeth found it difficult to create a stable government after the minsters who had served her so long died, notably William Cecil (Lord Burghley), Robert, Earl of Leicester, and Sir Francis Walsingham. Her arrogant favourite, Robert, Earl of Essex, proved a poor replacement. His lack of success against rebels in Ireland, where Elizabeth failed to allow an accommodating policy, led to his disgrace in 1599. Heavily in debt, Essex tried to stage a coup in order to seize Elizabeth and destroy his rival, the chief minister, Burghley's son, Sir Robert Cecil, who was Secretary of State from 1596 to 1608, thus bridging the reigns of Elizabeth and James I. The Cecils left copious archives, which were well looked after subsequently and ensures that their point of view is the most widely accessible.

The government had a stopgap feel to it by the late 1590s, in part due to Elizabeth's apparently imminent death. Essex sought to end an apparent impasse. In an impetuous and mistaken act of heroic chivalry, he wanted to force his way into Elizabeth's presence, overcoming the prohibition on his doing so, and then to make himself a key advisor. This was a position and a means she

---

Showing the Royal Past

Shakespeare is the most famous commentator on English monarchy, and to his list of plays may be added *The Reign of King Edward The Third* (1595), but he was not alone as a play-wright of past English monarchy. George Peele's patriotic *Edward I*, written in about 1590, appears to have been popular, at least in terms of the number of performances, which is a good indication. Christopher Marlowe provided *The Troublesome Reign and Lamentable Death of Edward the Second King of England*, a powerful play printed in 1594, the year after Michael Drayton's poem about Edward's favourite, *Piers Gaveston*. Thomas Heywood tackled the reign of Edward IV in *Edward IV, Parts I and II* (1599), a popular account that was reprinted in 1605, 1613, 1619 and 1626, and that, drawing on Holinshed's *Chronicles*, focused on Jane Shore, Edward's mistress, and her relationship with the king. The first part included a song about Agincourt.

---

was not prepared to accept. Six other peers supported Essex, but his attempt to raise the City of London in rebellion failed, and he was executed.

Essex had supported the revival of Tacitus, a Roman writer critical of imperial tyranny, a theme offered to the public in Ben Jonson's play *Sejanus* (1603 or 1604) about the Roman Emperor Tiberus's dominant minister. Henry Savile, translator of Tacitus, was a protégé of Essex, who may well have been guided by Tacitean concepts (derived from republican sympathies in the period of imperial Rome) of the need to resist tyrants and to drive out evil ministers. Yet Essex's attitude cut across the ethos of political order, respect for monarchy, and political prudence.

The theatre was involved in the politics of monarchy. John Hayward made much use of Tacitus and in 1600 was arrested and imprisoned for his *The First Part of the Life and Reign of Henry IV* (1599), which included the deposition of Richard II and was fulsomely dedicated to Essex. The Essex conspirators paid the Lord Chamberlain's Men, the company of actors with whom Shakespeare was linked, to revive his *Richard II*, including the deposition scene that had been prohibited in the published version. Elizabeth told William Lambarde soon after: 'I am Richard II, know you not that.' Her concern with her popularity led her in 1601 to give an audience to the MPs in which she spoke of her love for them. She was also well aware of her image, carefully managing how she was depicted in portraits, while her long reign helped in the fixing of Court ceremonies, albeit for an unmarried monarch.

Despite the problems of her last years, Elizabeth achieved much simply by hanging on, entrenching a period of civil peace after the Northern Rising of 1569 that contrasted with the French Wars of Religion. An increasing percentage of the population had been educated in a Protestant England and fewer had lived in an unchallenged world of Catholicism.

Elizabeth Recalled

In his *Letters from a Persian in England* (1735), George Lyttelton, a Whig politician, praised Elizabeth as the acme of governance: 'She was the head of this well-proportioned body, and supremely directed all its motions.' James I and Charles I were presented as seeking to make themselves 'absolute', but a system of limited royal power was seen as the product of the Glorious Revolution:

'Elizabeth chose to rule by Parliaments, from the goodness of her understanding; but princes now are forced to do so from necessity; because all expedients of governing without them are manifestly impracticable.'

Written in 1562–5, but published in 1583, Sir Thomas Smith's *De Republica Anglorum: the Manner of Government or Policy of the Realm of England* described England as a mixed government, and therefore not a tyranny, but was also clear about the authority of the Crown: 'the prince is the life, the head and the authority of all things that be done in the realm of England'. Elizabeth had been able to rule accordingly. Yet, the many difficulties of the last years of the reign, the section after the Spanish Armada, more than hinted at the many crises that the seventeenth century was to bring for monarchy, not only in England but also in Scotland.

4

Seventeenth-Century Crises

....

The Stuarts were the most unsuccessful of dynasties, with two of the monarchs driven from their thrones. Partly as a result, their reigns saw the development of constitutional and political parameters for the monarchy that were to prove of lasting significance.

JAMES I

When James VI of Scotland went south to claim his new, second crown in 1603, the transition to holding two was managed with far less difficulty than had been anticipated. There were problems, but nothing like the crisis accompanying the succession of the Bourbon dynasty in France in 1589. Arriving in London, James faced a conspiracy to assassinate him and put his first cousin, Lady Arbella Stuart, on the throne, but, betrayed by the intended recipient, the conspirators were seized.

James stayed in England for the rest of his reign, except for one visit back to Scotland, and he never went to Wales or Ireland. He was therefore less exposed than his Scottish predecessors to the impact of quarrels between Scottish lords, or to their defiance of royal authority, an exposure underlined by the Gowrie Plot in 1600, which probably involved an attempt to kidnap if not kill James. Scotland, however, remained an independent state, governed by the Scottish Privy Council and with a separate parliament.

Despite contemporary interest in the example of the union of Poland and Lithuania, and James's hopes for a 'union of love', or, at least, a measure of administrative and economic union between England and Scotland, the union remained essentially personal. There was fear in England about the legal and constitutional implications, and the Westminster Parliament rejected a parliamentary or legal bond. The union of Portugal and Spain was similarly personal. Yet, earlier, with James's accession peaceful and the Irish rebellion defeated, the king appeared to present success and stability, and notably so after the suppression of the Gunpowder Plot in 1605.

James, Shakespeare's second monarch, proved a figure whom it was difficult to incorporate into heroic accounts of kingship. As ruler both in Scotland and in England – a success that had eluded his predecessors in both kingdoms, and that represented a major triumph for the Stuart dynasty – James, nevertheless, lacked charisma and he found it difficult to win respect or affection, lacking, for example, the popularity later seen with Queen Anne (1702–14). As *Henry V* chronologically succeeded *Henry IV, Parts I and II*, the dissolute Prince Hal was shown by Shakespeare as rising to the occasion and to the need for majesty, when he came to the throne as Henry V. However, there was to be no such clear transition for James in 1603.

A Difficult Marriage

Although Anne of Denmark bore James seven children and had several miscarriages, the initially warm relationship became less so, and by the time she moved to England in 1603 it was poor. From 1607, they rarely lived together. Her chaplain, Godfrey Goodman, wrote:

> 'The King himself was a very chaste man, and there was little in the Queen to make him uxorious; yet they did love as well as man and wife could do, not conversing together.'

Anne's growing sympathy with Catholicism towards the end of her life was also an issue.

James was certainly well-educated, well-read, perceptive, thoughtful and conciliatory, as well as complex and self-indulgent. His considerable range of interests included witchcraft. James also had a menagerie that included an armadillo, while the gift of a snow leopard in 1611 was made problematic by the latter attacking a 'white red-deer calf'.

James's conciliatory, albeit stubborn, character, and his appreciation of the constraints of his position, helped limit religious tensions. More generally, presenting himself as moderate, James castigated opponents as extremists. Yet, his very different self-images included an authoritarian Constantinian image which had little time for opposition, this image linked to his commonplace stress on royal authority as having a religious role. With his emphasis on authority, James therefore offered a model of sacral kingship which paralleled that on the Continent, including in Catholic states. At the same time, he was interested in other writers and could be receptive to their arguments. The Methodist John Wesley, in his *History of England*, was to praise James for trying to preserve peace, but also offered an anachronistic view of what a king should be, one that spoke more to the reign of George III. Wesley thought that James's:

> failings were mostly owing to his being too early initiated in the intrigues of parties, who vied with each other to give him wrong notions of government, and to inspire him with a thorough hatred of all liberty, either civil or religious. Had he behaved upon his throne, and towards his subjects, as a plain, country gentleman would have acted towards his tenants upon his private estate, without launching into the subtleties of controversy, or pretending to explore the depths of politics, he would have made a great figure on the theatre of the world.

With James, the contrast between image, indeed what was to be seen as the 'Divine Right of Kings', and reality was more abrupt and harsher than with Elizabeth. The bisexual and spendthrift king presided over a corrupt and sleazy Court which did little to foster the prestige of either James or the monarchy, or to win support for his policies. As he was no warrior king, and preferred to pursue controversy in print, for example in favour of the divine right of kings, on which he also spoke to Parliament in 1609, James did not gain glory through victory. None of the Biblical models of kingship was truly present in James. The range of associations offered by James's kingship both provided multiple and conflicting contexts for Shakespeare's plays, and ensured that these plays could be seen as supportive or critical or disengaged with aspects of this kingship.

The Gunpowder Plot of 1605 is the headline event in James's reign, although the King James version of the Bible printed in 1611, in which James took much interest, was a more important lasting legacy. The plot, which cemented the view of Catholics as the enemy, was the culmination of a series of conspiracies relating to power and religion before, with and after James's accession, as hopes were advanced and thwarted. In general, religious tension diminished, helped by the end of war with Spain in 1604, a measure in line with Elizabethan policy, and by James's attempts to lessen differences between Protestants, although that was not how Puritans saw it. At the Hampton Court Conference of 1604, James allowed theologians of various Protestant views to participate. He himself had strong views on religious observance and on appropriate behaviour on Sundays, and backed moderate church reform, as well as being interested in the reunion of Christendom or, at least, of Protestantism and Catholicism. In 1619, James unsuccessfully attempted to mediate in the European crisis. His diplomacy in part arose from his search for a Christian reunion, which was linked to a desire for peace. The former entailed a wish for an ecumenical church council.

In the Gunpowder Plot, however, a small group of Catholics had put gunpowder in the cellars under Parliament, planning to blow it up when James opened the session on 5 November 1605, and hoping that the destruction of the royal family and the Protestant élite would ignite rebellion. The Gunpowder plotters aimed to kill James and Prince Henry in the explosion; James's nine-year-old daughter Elizabeth was to succeed and be brought up as a Catholic. The attempt to warn a Catholic peer, William, 4th Baron Monteagle, to be absent, led to the exposure of the plot. Seized with the gunpowder, Guy Fawkes was tortured (a vicious process) to reveal the names of his co-conspirators, and then brutally executed. A number of conspirators, including Robert Catesby, died resisting arrest. Henry Percy, 9th Earl of Northumberland, was sent to the Tower and held there until 1621, although his crime was Catholicism rather than conspiracy.

The bisexual James was keen on a series of pretty and greedy young men. This fondness had serious political implications because of his willingness to promote them into the aristocracy and at Court. In what became a major scandal, one favourite, Robert Carr, Earl of Somerset, and his wife were found guilty of poisoning Sir Thomas Overbury in the Tower of London in 1613, but were reprieved by James. Overbury knew too much about the seamy side of Court intrigues. Another unpopular and greedy favourite, George Villiers, the handsome son of a minor gentleman, became Royal Cupbearer in 1614, a Gentleman of the Bedchamber in 1615, Master of the Horse and a Viscount in 1616, and Duke of Buckingham in 1623, only to be assassinated in 1628 in the next reign.

A challenge to this style of the court was that of James's eldest son, Prince Henry, who became Prince of Wales in 1610, notably with an impressive parliamentary installation that was popularly seen as a quasi-coronation. Henry offered the muscular kingship that James conspicuously lacked, was a keen supporter of Protestantism, and also a patron of the arts, and was linked to the world of theatre himself, taking the lead role in Ben Jonson's masque *Oberon, the Fairy Prince* (1611). From 1603 to 1612, the Admiral's Men, the principal rivals of Shakespeare's company of players, were known as Prince Henry's Men. However, Henry, who would have been Henry IX, predeceased his father in 1612, dying of typhoid, and thus sparing his reputation the shock of the experience of rule. He was one of the many might-have-been monarchs removed by death, including the elder sons of Henry VII and Edward VII as well as William, son of Henry I in the *White Ship*. Charles therefore became one of the many younger sons succeeding to the throne. There were also the successions of young grandsons, due to the death of sons before their fathers, notably Richard II and George III.

Despite attaining the greater wealth of the English Crown, James lived beyond his means and could not avoid mounting debts. His policies were mistrusted. In a classic mismatch, he did not understand the character of Parliament, while MPs did not greatly appreciate his views. However, although the Addled Parliament of 1614 proved acrimonious and short, James acquired a degree of competence in the difficult management of English parliamentary and religious politics, as he had earlier done with the harder world of Scottish factionalism. In England and Scotland, there was no breakdown of control or stability akin to those in France and the Holy Roman Empire (Germany) in the 1610s and early 1620s. Nevertheless, James's reign helped bring the issue of Britishness forward, both politically and culturally, and very differently from the situation under Mary, Queen of Scots. Britishness, consciousness that drew in part on Welsh identity, posed difficulties, notably with Ireland in the 1590s and early 1600s. Thanks to crises for British-level policies of Anglicisation as well as local policies of a new order, first in Scotland in the late 1630s and then in Ireland in 1641, Britishness was to help provoke political breakdown across the British Isles as a whole.

The death of Prince Henry left the way clear for his less flexible and intelligent brother, Charles, who became Charles I in 1625, with many claiming that Buckingham had murdered James in order to make way for his friend. There was no evidence for this charge, and James had been seriously ill for months, but the claim reflected the uneasiness about Court life that was to the fore. In part, this was a matter of concern about Spanish influence, concern that looked back to the reign of Mary in the 1550s and to the conspiracies against Elizabeth. Buckingham had unsuccessfully backed a Spanish marriage for Charles, the two men going to Madrid to that end in 1623. In the event, Philip IV of Spain refused. Charles did make a Catholic marriage, soon after his accession, but with Henrietta Maria, a French princess, the sister of Louis XIII. This was far less wise than James's 1589 marriage to Anne of Denmark, a Protestant, and therefore an appropriate choice given Scottish politics at that juncture. James meanwhile had been hit hard by arthritis, gout and kidney stones in his last year. In March 1625, he had tertian ague or malaria, and then a stroke, finally dying during a devastating bout of dysentery.

James the Builder

The Banqueting House, built in 1619–22, was intended as the nucleus of a massive new palace in Whitehall. It was built by Inigo Jones who developed a classical architectural style. Fearful of assassination, James had disliked the colonnade in the previous hall on the site. Commissioned by Charles I and painted by Peter Paul Rubens in the early 1630s, the ceiling displayed the 'Apotheosis of James' seen being borne to Heaven by Justice and depicted as the heir of King Arthur and the monarch of universal peace. Charles was presented by Rubens as God's representative on Earth. The Banqueting House provided a venue for the public to see the king and the royal family eat, tickets being issued for admission. Charles was to be beheaded on a platform erected alongside the west side.

CHARLES I

Charles's early years saw unsuccessful war and problems with Parliament, a combination that had been seen since the thirteenth century. Indeed, there was more generally a strong sense of historicism in the criticism of Charles. Thus, with the Petition of Right (1628) drawing on Magna Carta (1215), the legacy of the challenge to John was applied to Charles in a way that would lack resonance today. There was also a major revival of ringing bells in celebration for the anniversary of the accession of Elizabeth, which recalled a past identification of the monarch with what were generally seen as national interests. This was a criticism of Charles.

The situation eased in the early 1630s, as a result of the murder of Charles's favourite, the Duke of Buckingham, in 1628 as well as of the coming of peace with France (1629) and Spain (1630). Nevertheless, Charles lacked common sense, was untrustworthy and could be harsh towards critics. He was authoritarian, intolerant and no compromiser. Prerogative courts under royal control, especially Star Chamber and High Commission, could give out savage penalties.

Charles's attitudes and policies contributed greatly to a polarisation of positions. The toleration of Catholics at court, where the French Catholic queen, Henrietta Maria, was a prominent supporter, was (unfairly) linked by critics to the Arminian tendency within the Church of England associated with William Laud, whom Charles made Archbishop of Canterbury in 1633. Laud sought to seal off the Church of England from Puritanism and Calvinism, but, under Laud, the Church's ritual element was seen as Catholic. Charles, a keen supporter of these religious policies, also sought to maintain the dignity of kingship. In this, he followed James, but in a different context.

Nevertheless, despite differences over constitutional questions, such as the relationship between the monarch and the law, few in England wished to overthrow Charles. There was considerable public attachment to the role of Parliament and to the principle of parliamentary taxation, but the system of government was generally believed to be divinely instituted, and it was felt that, if Charles was a bad ruler, God would punish him in the next world, not man in this. Although religion was seen by some as providing justification for resistance, rebellion and civil war were regarded by most as akin to plagues in the body of the nation, and looked far from predictable in the mid-1630s.

The outbreak of civil war in England was the immediate result of political crisis in 1641–2 stemming from risings in Scotland (1638) and Ireland (1641). Indeed, the crisis that engulfed Charles was bound up with the fact that the Stuarts ruled over a multiple kingdom, whereas the Hanoverian kings, in 1715–16, 1745–6 and 1798, were to overcome crises that stemmed from the same cause. In Wales, there was criticism of the policies of Charles I in the 1620s and 1630s, and in particular of the activities of the Council of the Marches, but it was far less serious than that elsewhere. In Scotland, the absentee Charles's support for a stronger episcopacy and a new liturgy, and his tactless and autocratic handling of Scottish interests and patronage, not least on his visit to Scotland in 1633, led to a Presbyterian and national response which produced a National Covenant (1638) opposed to all ecclesiastical innovations unless they were agreed by the General Assembly.

Instead of compromising, Charles stood firm. In the Bishops' Wars (1639–40) his folly of threatening violence in 1639 was followed by trying to make good that threat in 1640 without the means to sustain it. Charles made a poor choice of commanders, and inadequate finance wrecked logistics. The English army was poorly prepared and deployed, and therefore collapsed when attacked by the large and professionally officered Scottish army.

As with the last military commitment, the wars with Spain and France of the 1620s, the Bishops' Wars weakened Charles, first by undermining his finances, and then because he was unsuccessful. They also altered the relationship between Crown and Parliament in England. Charles's 'Personal Rule' had failed because of events. Rulers of England lacked the resources to fight wars, unless they turned to Parliament. To raise funds, Charles summoned the 'Short Parliament' in April 1640, but, with the opposition being unhelpful, it refused to vote on taxes until grievances had been redressed, and was speedily dissolved. That October, the Treaty of Ripon ended the Bishops' Wars, but left the Scots in occupation of the North of England and in receipt of a daily payment by Charles until a final settlement could be negotiated. Charles was therefore forced to turn to Parliament again, and this 'Long Parliament', which met that November, was to survive, albeit with many and serious interruptions and changes of membership, until 1660: longer, in fact, than Charles.

Initially, Parliament was united in the redress of grievances and represented a sense of national identity and interest beside which the king's views appeared unacceptable. Parliament used the weapon of impeachment against Charles's much-feared ministers. Thomas, 1st Earl of Strafford, the autocratic Lord Deputy of Ireland, was attainted and executed in 1641 for planning to bring Charles's Irish army to England, and Laud, abandoned by Charles, was imprisoned (he was executed in 1645). The theme of an Irish army brought to England was to be a recurring one in the seventeenth century.

Restrictions on the Crown's power were even more important, and Charles's opponents thought them crucial. One, Lord Saye and Sele, subsequently wrote that it was necessary to resist Charles because he had determined 'to destroy the Parliament of England'. The opponents wanted to restore what they saw as the government of Elizabeth I: a system of clearcut Protestantism at home and abroad, and both Parliament and the aristocracy through the Privy Council playing a major role. A Triennial Act decreed that Parliament was to meet at least every three years.

Other Acts forbade the dissolution of the Long Parliament without its own consent, abolished Star Chamber, High Commission and Ship Money, and limited the Crown's financial power. Although these measures raised contentious points, while the obstinate Charles was hostile after the execution of Strafford, these changes were accomplished without causing the division that religious issues created at the end of 1641. As with the French Revolution, which was relatively harmonious in 1790, there was no immediate total breakdown.

In England in 1641 as in France in 1791, religion proved a key point of contention. The retention of episcopacy (bishops), traditional order and discipline in the Church proved very divisive in England and helped rally support for Charles. A Royalist party developed, in part due to the ability of the Crown to draw on a range of support but also handicapped by the disunity arising from the resulting range, for example between Protestants and Catholics. The resulting factionalism weakened Charles both prior to the war and, later, in the wartime conduct of the royal war effort.

The possible abolition of episcopacy was particularly divisive in relations with Parliament. Moreover, the need to raise forces to deal with a major Catholic rising in Ireland in 1641 led to a serious rift over how they were to be controlled. In an escalating crisis, Charles resorted to violence, invading Parliament on 4 January 1642 in order to seize his six most virulent opponents, including John Pym, but they had already fled by water to the City of London, a stronghold of hostility to the king. As both sides prepared for war, Charles left London on 10 January 1642 in order to raise forces. He was only to return as a captive.

Civil war did not find Charles a good commander, and when with the Royalist field army it could underperform, as at Naseby in 1645, although many factors were responsible for the fate of battle. Charles headed the social hierarchy, and his armies reflected this. Royalists were concerned mostly to defend the established order, and leadership for Charles was in large part a function of social position, with prominent roles for his nephew Prince Rupert of the Rhine and for Henry, 5th Earl of Worcester. Much (but crucially not all) of the peerage and gentry thought their position bound up with that of the king, and Charles and his supporters essentially relied on traditional notions of honour, obligation and loyalty to raise troops.

The defeated Charles gave himself up to the Scots in 1646, being handed over by them to the Parliamentarians in 1647. The fate of the king played a major role in negotiations, but Charles again backed the unsuccessful option. Having rejected Oliver Cromwell's proposed settlement of religious and political differences in 1647, Charles turned to the Scots, agreeing in the Engagement to introduce a Presbyterian system in return for a Scottish invasion on his behalf. This illustrated his duplicity, and was doomed by failure in the Second Civil War, that of 1648. As with his grandmother, Mary, Queen of Scots, in 1587, duplicity and failure were followed by decapitation.

The victorious army was determined to deal with Charles. Thanks to religious zeal, its leadership was not intimidated about confronting their anointed king. They saw him as a 'Man of Blood' who had killed the Lord's People. In order to stop Parliament from negotiating with Charles, the army purged Parliament in Pride's Purge on 6 December 1648. Those who were left, the 'Rump', appointed a court to try Charles for treason against the people. Parliament argued that Charles had given his word of honour not to fight again, and that he had broken it when he encouraged the Second Civil War. Charles refused to plead, arguing that subjects had no right to try the king and that he stood for the liberties of the people. He was found guilty and beheaded on 30 January 1649 at the centre of royal power, outside the Banqueting Hall in Whitehall.

The formal trial and public execution of Charles I were markedly dissimilar to the killing of medieval kings, as, in a culmination of theories of resistance, they were intended as the centrepiece of the end of monarchy. England was declared a republic, The Commonwealth, the regalia, which was allegedly left by Edward the Confessor, was destroyed and the House of Lords was abolished. Royal coats of arms and other devices were removed, and statues of Charles were destroyed. Royal emblems were replaced by the paired shields of England and Ireland, while Charles's Great Seal, which had depicted him, was destroyed and replaced with a map of England, Ireland and Wales. Richmond Palace was largely demolished and used for building materials.

The execution made compromise with the Royalists impossible, and was to continue to be highly controversial, with Charles becoming a martyr in the view of the Church of England. This perception has now been very largely lost, and Charles instead, an anachronistic opponent of change to many nineteenth-century liberal commentators, has been more recently presented as foolish. Yet, his earlier reputation underlines how monarchs, and, indeed monarchy, have been the foci for different views. Thus, Thomas Carte, a Jacobite, in his *A General History of England* (1755) described the king and the regicide in strongly religious terms:

[Charles] died a martyr for the liberties of his people, and the rights of the Church of England ... It can hardly be supposed that an iniquity of so enormous a size, as the murder of a rightful sovereign, whose virtues and piety entitled him to a crown of glory, shall pass unattended by some divine judgment.

Carte claimed that the regicide was responsible for the irreligion, immorality, and divisions of the nation to the present day and thus that it repeated in human time the Fall, that is, Adam's sin. More specifically, Carte argued that the regicide led to the future Charles II and James II going abroad, with all the detrimental consequences that followed from their being educated as Catholics.

The Rump regime was able to do well in war, with Charles II, who had been crowned in Scotland, defeated in 1650–1, and Scotland, Ireland and remaining Royalist overseas positions conquered and the Dutch defeated. However, the Rump could not settle serious divisions within the republican camp, and, in response, Cromwell, the commander-in-chief, seized power in 1653 and became Lord Protector.

This was a new form of monarchy, with much of the traditional ceremony including a coronation oath and enthronement. Cromwell lived in royal palaces with a Court, his coins displayed him with royal regalia, and he received the power to nominate his successor. However, having considered becoming king, Cromwell eventually pulled back from accepting the offer of the throne and stressed that he was 'ready to serve not as King but as Constable'.

Cromwell died in 1658 on the anniversary of his great victories of Dunbar (1650) and Worcester (1651), but he was not an Alexander the Great cut short in his prime. Cromwell had neither led the latter-day children of Israel to the promised land, as he had sought to do, nor created a stable government that would maintain and further his achievements. Cromwell's support for legal and educational reform was, however, forward-looking. Cromwell exploited the conflict between France and Spain in order to win the alliance of France which had hitherto supported the Royalists, but the war with Spain proved very costly. Christer Bonde, a Swedish ambassador who spoke good English and was friendly with Cromwell, reported: 'this regime is riddled with intrigues and with such jealousies that I have some reason to doubt whether there may not be those who deliberately confuse sensible policies so that matters may go ill'. When Cromwell died, the unpopularity and divisions of the regime were readily apparent, and there was, in Charles II, a legitimate pretender still threatening the stability of the system. Cromwell's successor as Protector, his pleasant but weak and ineffectual son, Richard, was unable to command authority, but, in his last months, Oliver's leadership had also been faltering.

Parliamentary, army and financial problems crippled Richard's protectorate. He crucially lacked the support of the army. Deposed in 1659 as a result of a military coup, he was followed by a restoration of the Rump Parliament and the Commonwealth, but the Parliament was dismissed by the army (October 1659), and, with anarchy apparently imminent and the army divided, the commander in Scotland, George Monck, marched south, and restored order and a moderate Parliament. Political instability, combined with the strains created by government policies, led to support for the return of monarchy which occurred in 1660. Charles II was invited to return from exile and did so in May, John Evelyn writing in his diary that 'it was the Lord's doing'.

CHARLES II

The Character of a King
'This Prince might more properly be said to have gifts than virtues, such as affability, easiness of living, inclinations to give and to forgive; qualities that flowed from his nature . . . One great objection made to him was the concealing himself, and disguising his thoughts.'

George, Marquess of Halifax of Charles II

Charles was an appropriate figure to preside over the reconciliation and, still more, the stabilisation required after the 1640s and 1650s. Crucially, Parliament and the Church of England were restored to what they had been organisationally before the Civil War. Able and determined on his rights, Charles was nevertheless flexible and his ambition was essentially modest, the preservation of his position, rather than centring on any creation of a strong monarchy. Although regarded as accessible, Charles II insisted on the dignity of kingship, not least in the shape of form and protocol. From 1673, political division in England was linked to a style at once grander in public but also more reserved in private. Yet, he lacked the autocratic manner of his cousin, Louis XIV of France, who assumed personal power in 1661. If there was to be a royalist reaction, it would not be led by the king, although it was claimed that he told his trusted advisors in 1669 that he planned an autocracy. Charles's charm was also a definite asset and, if he was not trusted by all, and was seen as a tyrant and a rake by some, he was able to avoid the reputations and fates of his father, Charles I, and his brother, James II and VII.

Charles II was unhappy with the religious settlement and with attempts to restrict his freedom of manoeuvre. These attempts became more serious as a result of his apparent Catholic lean- ings. He was the ruler on whom the fictional King Bolloximian, of *Sodom: or, the Quintessence of Debauchery*, was modelled:

Thus in the zenith of my lust I reign;

I eat to survive and survive to eat again
. . . And with my prick I'll govern all the land.

John Wesley was to think Charles 'abandoned to all vices. A worse man never sat on the English throne.'

Vice and corruption at court were bad enough, to many, but an alleged Catholic as ruler was totally unacceptable. In a culture that knew little of religious toleration, such a king appeared to imperil national independence, the Church and society. Anti-popery and fear of arbitrary government were as important in the second half of the century as in the first. Rumours about secret clauses in the Treaty of Dover with Louis XIV in 1670 soon leaked out, and suspicion about Charles's intentions bedevilled the remainder of his reign, testing the relationship between Crown and socio-political elite. In 1672, Charles issued a Declaration of Indulgence in which he claimed the prerogative right to vary the parliamentary settlement of religious affairs. He suspended the enforcement of the laws against worship by Dissenters and permitted Catholics to worship in their own homes. Such moves fanned fears about Charles, as did the stop on payments out of the Exchequer in 1672 and the joint attack with Louis XIV on the Dutch the same year, and, more generally, Charles's favour for Catholics at court.

Yet, as later with George III, it would be unwise to exaggerate the king's unpopularity. Charles touched a large number of people for the King's Evil (scrofula), many more than previous monarchs in order to emphasise his sacred kingship. Touching was evidence of popular faith in, and demand for, the curative powers of kingship. Moreover, Charles stood between the people and a return to both the anarchy of the 1640s and the military rule of the 1650s.

Although he was the father of at least fourteen male bastards, the succession was a major problem for Charles. There were no legitimate children by his marriage to the Portuguese princess, Catherine of Braganza (who had brought Bombay and Tangier as her dowry in 1661), so his brother James, Duke of York, was his heir. The Popish Plot of 1678 stemmed from false claims, made by the adventurer Titus Oates, of the existence of a Catholic plot to assassinate Charles and replace him with James. Such false claims were encouraged by rumours about the agreement actually reached at Dover in 1670, one in which negotiations were in part handled by Charles's sister Henrietta, Duchess of Orléans, wife to Louis XIV's brother. Charles agreed to an alliance with Louis and to convert to Catholicism, while Louis promised yearly payments as well as troops if there was a rebellion as a result.

Considerably more astute than his father, and helped by an absence of any equivalent of the earlier crises of 1638–41, Charles rode out the Popish Plot and the subsequent Exclusion Crisis of

1679–81, an attempt to determine the succession by excluding James that anticipated those following the eventual failure of James after he became king. Republicanism was no real option. It had been discredited by the execution of Charles I and its aftermath. Indeed, Royalist writers sought to damn Charles's opponents as republicans, for example Robert Brady's linkage of Presbyterians and sectarians as opponents of the monarchy in his *An Introduction to the Old English History* (1684). Whig opponents of the Crown sought to deny any linkage or republican sympathy. Yet, there were still republican arguments. They drew on Classical sources and political and religious stances, as in Henry Neville's highly controversial book *Plato Redivius* (1681).

JAMES II

Instead, the conflict remained in a monarchical context and, outmanoeuvring his parliamentary rivals, Charles regained control and built up the royal position in his last years. Moreover, James II (James VII in Scotland) was able to succeed in 1685 and to suppress risings in England and Scotland. As part of another War of the Succession, the Duke of Monmouth, an illegitimate son of Charles II, claimed the succession. Invading, Monmouth was defeated at Sedgemoor. He escaped that but, unlike Charles after his defeat at Worcester in 1651, was captured and executed.

Born in St James's Palace in 1633, baptised by Laud, and named after James I, James looked back to a world before the Civil War. Convinced of divine approval, James moved toward Catholicisation after Sedgemoor. In his speech opening the parliamentary session that November, James made it clear that he wanted both a large permanent army and, in violation of the Test Act, no limitation on his right to employ Catholic officers, declaring: 'there is nothing but a good force of well-disciplined troops in constant pay that can defend us from such as, either at home or abroad, are disposed to disturb us'. Parliament was opposed, whereupon James prorogued it. Parliament never met again in his reign, and he pressed ahead with its policies.

James's stance was challenged by the succession. He had two daughters, Mary and Anne, from his Protestant first marriage to Anne Hyde, with Mary married to James's nephew, William III of Orange, who was the leading Dutch political figure and a Protestant. His fifteen-year-long second, Catholic, marriage to Mary of Modena had yielded no surviving children. As a result, the birth of a Prince of Wales in June 1688 was a major upset. Critics spread the rumour that a baby had been smuggled into the queen's bed in a warming pan.

The more volatile situation combined with a move toward war in Western Europe. Keen to keep Britain out of the camp of his rival, Louis XIV of France, William of Orange, invited by the seven 'Immortals' of later Whig legend, invaded that November. William brought with him a substantial army as he expected a difficult campaign. However, he benefited from a collapse of will on the part of James, who had an army twice the size of William's. James had been a brave (mainly naval) commander earlier in his life, but in 1688 he suffered from a collapse of resolve and a series of debilitating nose-bleeds, and failed to lead his army into battle. There was also a haemorrhage of support, culminating with the flight of Lieutenant-General John Churchill from James's camp at Salisbury to William's side, and that of Princess Anne from London. In turn, William refused to halt his march on London in order to allow negotiations to proceed, as the Tory leaders, who were less unfavourable to James than were the Whigs, would have preferred. James fled the capital, throwing the Great Seal of England into the Thames. Fear of the London mob and of anarchy led to the Archbishop of Canterbury and leading peers taking control of the city. Captured and returned to London, where his presence obstructed the creation of a new political and constitutional order, James was finally driven abroad by Dutch pressure.

Had James prevailed, as he had against Monmouth, then he would have been able to remould the political system, using the force he controlled, and ensuring that it was better funded. This would have matched comparable governmental developments on the Continent, and led to a British version of the system described as absolutism. Victory for James in 1688 would have cemented the reaction against Parliament in Charles's last years. Abroad, James would probably have allied with Louis XIV, whereas William declared war on him in May 1689. In exile, James took part in plots for his restoration, but they were doomed by English naval power, and notably so in 1692. James saw these as signs of a lack of providential support, and spent much time in devotion.

In 1697, as a condition of peace, Louis recognised William III, and in 1701 James died of a brain haemorrhage, but at the age of sixty-seven, a good age for the period. Buried in the Church of the English Benedictines in Paris, his tomb was looted during the French Revolution, being rebuilt from 1828 in accordance with a commission by George IV. By then, the main line of the Stuarts had come to an end. James II had had one son, 'James III', James Francis Edward Stuart who claimed the throne until his death in 1766. He in turn had two sons, Charles Edward Stuart, or Bonnie Prince Charlie, who claimed the throne until he died without legitimate issue in 1788, and then his younger brother, Henry, or Henry IX, a Cardinal, who died childless in 1807.

WILLIAM III

A vacuum of power had been created in the winter of 1688–9 within the context of a Dutch occupation that drew on significant English support. Most people did not want any breach in the hereditary succession, not only because of the example of 1649 but also due to a belief that civil power came from God, and William had initially claimed that he had no designs on the

Crown. However, as the situation developed favourably for him, especially when James had been driven into exile, William made it clear that he sought the throne. This was achieved in 1689 by declaring it vacant, a legal fiction based on James's flight from London being depicted as an abdication, and inviting William and Mary to occupy it as joint monarchs. All Catholics were debarred from the succession. In short, however much government derived its authority from God, the exercise of this authority and the type of government were left to humans. In 1660 and 1689, the action was very clearly human, and indeed in effect a rump of Parliament acted as kingmaker.

1689 saw an innovation redolent of medieval solutions: joint monarchy. William III became king with his wife co-ruler as Mary II. That could have led to a new Anglo-Dutch ruling family, an outcome encouraged by William's role as royal warrior in 1688–90. In 1690, he was in command when James was defeated at the battle of the Boyne, which was swiftly followed by the capture of Ireland. Thereafter, William returned to his earlier focus on resisting the French advance in the Low Countries, now with the benefit of British forces. Indeed, he won additional prestige by regaining Namur in 1695. In Nicholas Rowe's play *Tamerlane* (1701), the protagonist of Christopher Marlowe's 1587 play was reworked to appear as William III, with his eventually defeated Ottoman (Turkish) rival Bajazet as Louis XIV.

However, there was to be no dynastic continuity as William and Mary had no children. Anne's rights in the succession had been subordinated to those of William, so that, when Mary died of smallpox in 1694, the joint monarchy was succeeded by William ruling alone, and Anne did not come to the throne until 1702 when William died childless. The provision, in the Bill of Rights, that Anne and her issue should come before any issue of William from a second marriage was not necessary.

There was also a major shift in the nature of monarchy in Scotland, where the Convention of the Estates declared the throne forfeit. The contractual nature of the Revolution Settlement, the extent to which the Crown had been obtained by William and Mary on conditions, was far more apparent in Scotland than in England. The offer of the Crown to William and Mary was made conditional on their acceptance of the Claim of Right issued by the Scottish Convention, which stated that James VII had forfeited the Crown by his policies and that no Catholic could become ruler of Scotland, nor hold public office. The Scottish Parliament also gained greater independence from William than from his predecessors. The degree of radicalism in the Scottish constitutional settlement, which included the disestablishment of the Scottish Episcopalian Church, reflected fundamentally different political circumstances from those in England, including the far greater impact of William's wishes in the latter.

Both short- and long-term circumstances were significant in the Scottish case. The pattern of restrictions on the Crown was far more entrenched, in part due to the reaction against Mary, Queen of Scots but, more consistently, as a result of the lack of automatic aristocratic support for monarchy, a situation that reflected long-standing contentious factional domestic politics.

The financial settlement for the Crown in England left William with an ordinary revenue that was small for his peacetime needs, obliging him to turn to Parliament for support. The Civil List in effect made rulers employees of the state. Moreover, a standing (permanent) army was prohibited unless permitted by Parliament. This was a key limitation on royal power that reflected anger with James's policies. William had to accept the discipline of parliamentary monarchy: regular meetings of Parliament, which in effect ended the right to call and dismiss Parliament at will in that another would have to be called, frequent elections, and reliance on ministers who could manage Parliament and state finances. The last was a longstanding requirement but now one that was more urgent. There were ten elections between 1695 and 1715. However, the extent to which William was still able to impose his views indicated his political importance as the arbitrator of both Court factionalism and the ministerial struggle for influence. This role was not really compromised by the emergence of political parties, because they lacked the structure and ethos necessary to provide clear leadership and agreed policy, and certainly did so until the 1700s when such groups became more coherent and, therefore, effective.

The public presentation of William drew on established themes, notably those of royal warrior and Protestant hero. Thus, Antonio Verrio's murals on the King's Staircase at Hampton Court glorified William as Alexander the Great. Yet there was a change in the assessment of monarchy, one that looked toward the present situation. From the late seventeenth century, there was a move away from the Baroque sensibilities and themes that had characterised the presentation of rulers and rulership, past as well as present, fictional as well as factual. These sensibilities and themes had looked back to the presentation of rulers by Classical as well as Christian writers, a process brought together anew by Renaissance Humanists as they sought to extol past and present Western rulers with reference to Classical forbears. From the Reformation and Counter-Reformation, this approach had come with an older, stronger sense of the monarch as defender of the Church. It brought with it the idea of the monarch as the embodiment of the national religion.

However, from the late seventeenth century, in part as a reaction to Absolutism, both British and Continental, and in part as a product of a more utilitarian approach to rulership, there was more of an emphasis on specific factors in the assessment of particular rulers. A focus on factual analysis, on observation rather than traditional authority, a focus in line with the intellectual prospectus offered by Francis Bacon and René Descartes, was intended to provide a more realistic account. Linked to this, the understanding and presentation of truth moved from moral precepts to the search for specific facts, and a concern with origins and development led to an interest in change. The idea of constant attributes, very much related to the 'humours' of the individual, was replaced by one that provided opportunities to understand change in terms of success and failure, and, linked to this, of an interplay of circumstances and character. In a reaction against what he saw as irrational, William refused to touch for the King's Evil, although Anne was to do so later. His was a monarchy that had some links with the self-conscious rationality termed 'political arithmetic,' as well as with the Scientific Revolution, which encouraged a sense that predictable rules or laws existed in the natural world. The understanding of monarchy in the century after the Glorious Revolution of 1688 reflected the growing impact of the ideas of balance linked to the Newtonian exposition of mechanistic physics. Understanding the state in these terms meant an approach to monarchy as part of a well-ordered system rather than as a sacral intermediary with God. The religious dimension continued but in this new context.

The new style of perception was also related to a reportage that reflected the rise of the press, with, in England, the end of pre-publication censorship in 1695 followed in 1701 by the *Daily Courant*, the first daily newspaper. Moreover, the interplay between the Crown and adversarial parliamentary politics furthered attention to the monarch as a changing individual.

In 1702, as in 899, 1100, 1199, 1307, 1399, 1603 and 1901, there was the near-coincidence of a change of monarch with the arbitrary organisation of time in terms of a new century. That can be helpful, even if, or especially because, there is not necessarily a major shift, still less a change in dynasty. The death of William III was important because it brought to an end the prospect of an Anglo-Dutch ruling house. There was to be the marriage in 1734 of George II's eldest daughter, Anne, with William IV of Orange, and the Orange interest was strongly backed by the British in key moments in Dutch factional polity in 1747 and 1787. However, William IV was a cousin of William III with no claim on the British succession. His son, William V (1748–1806), driven out by French Revolutionary forces in 1795, spent his last years in exile at Kew, as in effect a cadet British prince, grandson of George II.

The latter's father, George I, had brought about a very different foreign link. As with William III, however, this could be presented in terms of a national continuity guaranteed by Parliament. Indeed, Classical references appeared most appropriate for monarchy after 1688, not in a republican context, but, rather, with reference to a new monarchical destiny, first with William and later with George. Each could be discussed as a new Augustus, a figure who would bring peace and stability after division, conflict and chaos. While correctly suggesting that William and George were not Cromwells, they also earned fame by the comparison.

Given the significance of the Glorious Revolution, William's reputation was readily drawn into subsequent political disputes. Thus, on 1 January 1732, the *Weekly Register*, a London Whig paper, published 'An answer to the infamous libel on the memory of the late King William, printed in *Fog's Journal* of Saturday last', an answer that included the justified claim that he 'set a bound to the conquests of Lewis the Great' [Louis XIV]. There was also controversy in Bristol in the 1730s as to whether to erect a statue to William. Yet, although praise for Arthur, Alfred and Elizabeth I reflected a determination by many to offer a native stance to monarchy, the incorporation of foreigners from 1603 on had been a successful one. Anglicisation might not be enough to please critics, some of them well-informed, but foreign-born monarchs now had to accept the principles and exigencies of parliamentary monarchy. This indeed was the very basis of the right to the throne enjoyed by the monarchs from 1689, and, more particularly, with the Hanoverian dynasty that came to the throne in 1714 in the person of George I.

William as Royal Palace-builder

At Hampton Court and Kensington, William demolished earlier work and built essentially new palaces, both carefully integrated with their gardens. Sir Christopher Wren remodelled Hampton Court for William with scant concern for the Tudor fabric: he designed the Baroque Fountain Court which was surrounded by two sets of state rooms, because William was a joint monarch with Mary II. As a consequence, there were two royal staircases and so on. The enfilade of the king's state rooms was designed to exalt William, not simply with the three throne rooms, but also with the large state bed. On the ground floor, William's living quarters were far more modest, as was in keeping both with his character and with the emphasis on display under the public gaze.

A palace nearer London was also required, and, with Whitehall unacceptable because its damp exacerbated William's asthma, he bought the Earl of Nottingham's house in Kensington for £20,000 and had that greatly altered, not least with a series of reception rooms. Queen Anne added an Orangery to Kensington, and George I work on the state rooms and garden.

5

Eighteenth-Century Settlement

....

Treating the subject in terms of a rough century links Anne (1702–14) to George I, II and III, and, conversely, George IV and William III to Victoria. This has value in terms of underlining the extent of continuity between dynasties, which indeed explained their succession. The process also encourages a rethinking of transition markers. In the case of Anne, a key one was parliamentary Union with Scotland in 1707, a link related to the Act of Succession in 1701. Anne had seventeen pregnancies from her 1683 marriage to Prince George of Denmark, but none of her five children survived to adulthood, which was a very different reason for dynastic discontinuity than William and Mary's childlessness or Charles II's failure to have legitimate children. The death in 1701 of the most long-lived of Anne's children, William, Duke of Gloucester, at the age of eleven, led to a need to clarify the succession which resulted in the Act of Settlement. This provided for the succession of the Electoral house of Hanover, the claim of which derived from the daughter of James VI and I, Elizabeth. In 1613, she had married Frederick V, Elector Palatine, the short-lived king of Bohemia in the early stages of the Thirty Years' War (1618–48); as a result of which Elizabeth was known as the Winter Queen. Their youngest daughter, Sophia (1630–1714) married Ernst August of the north German Protestant princely house of Brunswick-Luneburg and the future George I was the eldest of their large family of six boys and one girl. Moreover, the joint inheritance of Ernst August and his brothers shaped the Duchy of Hanover which, in 1692, became one of the electorates of the Holy Roman Empire.

ANNE

Born in 1665, Anne died aged forty-nine. Poor health greatly reduced her vigour, which was far less than that of Elizabeth (1741–62) and Catherine II (the Great, 1762–96) of Russia. As Anne, although a devout Anglican, had no domestic programme of change, she was a relatively uncontroversial figure, and political criticism in her reign centred on ministers, not monarch. Her options were also constrained by the degree to which her reign was lived in the shadow of war, although, in 1708, she was the last British ruler to veto an Act of Parliament, that of the Scottish Militia Bill, which, however, did not produce a crisis. The notion of mixed monarchy and king in Parliament was long-established.

Anne's reign saw many instances of the habitual pattern of comparing monarchs, and, in her case, the obvious comparison was with Elizabeth I. This might now seem implausible, but it did not at the time, and the comparison was made not only in publications but also in correspondence, Sir John Chardin, a prominent merchant, writing in 1703:

> The reign of the Queen proves as successful, glorious, and beloved as that of the renowned Elizabeth and England saw nothing like since her in point of reciprocal confidence and love between the sovereign and the people, and her Majesty's reign is like to be as fatal to the King of France [Louis XIV] as the other to the King of Spain [Philip II].

There was also a political point. Supporters of intervention in Continental politics, as under Anne, cited Elizabeth's backing for the Dutch Revolt from 1585. More fancifully, the play *Zelmane: or*

The Corinthian Queen (1705) made a direct comparison between the protagonist, an able war leader, and Anne.

Yet, Anne was able and also not as dependent on her favourites, notably Sarah Churchill, Duchess of Marlborough, as was believed by some contemporaries, and, as such, was subsequently to become an historical orthodoxy. Indeed, her role was to be unduly minimised, for the role of the monarch as arbitrator was amply demonstrated by Anne's continued importance in the struggle for primacy at Court and among her ministers. Furthermore, Anne had personal popularity with churchmen in particular, but also the wider population.

An instructive change arose from the re-placing of the monarchy in London. Whitehall had been the centre of power over the previous two centuries, at once royal palace and the place of government. However, in 1698, fire destroyed the palace and only the Banqueting Hall remained. Despite proposals, Whitehall was not rebuilt as a palace. Instead, the monarchs focused Court life on smaller palaces: St James's, Kensington, Hampton Court, and Buckingham. These, however, were not appropriate as centres of a governing process that was growing in scale. Instead of remaining with the Court, administration was rehoused in new buildings on the Whitehall site which linked civil servants to ministers and kept both physically close to Parliament. The perception and reality of royal power was affected, as, at times, the Crown could appear tangential to this new nexus, or, at best, part of a more multi-faceted governmental process. This was indeed the case, but separating government out made the situation more apparent.

The role of Parliament was also enhanced by the union of the Edinburgh and Westminster parliaments in 1707, the sequel to the personal union achieved in 1603 when James VI of Scotland became James I of England. The 1707 Union was an aspect of history about monarchy rather than of it. The Union reflected anxiety that England and Scotland would go for different options when Anne died, and tensions over the possibility of a different Scottish foreign policy. Anne's ministers, rather than Anne herself, were the key players.

Indeed, a sense of change from earlier Stuart policy was captured in a parliamentary speech of 1710 by Robert Walpole, a prominent Whig MP and later, from 1721 to 1742, foreign minister, supporting the impeachment of the Tory High-Churchman Henry Sacheverell. Walpole drew a clear contrast between what he saw as the pre-1688 Stuart doctrine of monarchy and the post-Revolution situation. This contrast helps explain how Whigs responded to what they subsequently perceived as unwelcome royal initiatives:

> The doctrine of unlimited, unconditional passive obedience [to a monarch] was first invented to support arbitrary and despotic power ... What then can be the designs of preaching this doctrine now, unasked, unsought for, in her Majesty's reign, where the law is the only rule and measure of the power of the Crown, and of the obedience of the people.

Walpole was soon after sent to the Tower but that was due to Anne's Tory ministers, not the queen.

House of Hanover

Under the Act of Settlement of 1701, the Hanoverian rulers would have to take coronation oaths committing them to rule 'according to the statutes in Parliament agreed', and to maintain the Protestant religion as established by law. The Hanoverians, however, came to claim a hereditary right via Matilda, daughter of Henry II and wife of Henry the Lion, Duke of Saxony. In 1701, a medal was struck at the request of Electress Sophia of Hanover, granddaughter of James I and mother of George I, to mark her being named heiress to the Crown of England. The reverse depicted 'Matilda [c. 1156–1189], daughter of Henry II, King of England, wife of Henry the Lion . . . mother of Emperor Otto IV . . . Progenitor of the House of Brunswick.' This medal grounded the Hanoverian claim on the succession in primogeniture and the history of the House of Guelph, and not on the Act of Settlement passed by Parliament in 1701. It was a claim also advanced by John Wesley in his *Concise History of England* in 1775, in which he traced the legitimacy of the Hanoverian succession back to Matilda. History thereby served to establish and strengthen an alternative claim. Pro-Hanoverian English historians, such as Laurence Echard, also focused on this argument. Such dynastic locating was scarcely new, but it remained important. Indeed, dynastic history was not only a traditional theme in England, and one that was crucial to state-formulation, but was also pushed to the fore by the related challenge posed by Jacobite claims, or believed to be posed by them.

Yet the hereditary argument on behalf of the Hanoverians had no weight in Britain. Instead, legislation of 1689 and 1701 ensured that there was a degree of elective character to British kingship but also grounded the kingship in a parliamentary dispensation designed to ensure permanence.

Prince George of Hanover became a naturalised British subject in 1705 and Duke of Cambridge the following year. But Anne saw his presence as a challenge to her royal majesty and a reminder of her mortality. In April 1714, she responded angrily to Sophia's attempt to have George summoned to take his seat in the House of Lords as Duke of Cambridge. There was speculation that the Tories would try to ensure the succession for 'James III', but, when Anne died in August 1714, having to her satisfaction outlived Sophia, all passed peacefully, largely as a result of inadequate Jacobite preparations and a lack of foreign support. Sophia had died, aged eighty-four, that June; and George I therefore succeeded.

GEORGE I

A taciturn and reserved figure, George (1714–27), has been posi-
tively re-evaluated in recent decades, notably by Ragnhild Hatton,
which is a reminder of how an individual historian can play a
major role in the reputation of an individual monarch. Yet, George
bears much of the responsibility for a terrible breakdown in relations with his son in 1717 as well as for committing Britain to a
risky and expensive international posture that led to war with
Spain in 1718–20 and, in 1720, as a result of pursuing Hanoverian
interests, nearly resulted in conflict with Peter the Great of Russia.

George suffered from the difficulty of learning to adjust to his
new role. The nature of politics was very different from that in
Hanover, and the conduct politicians thought appropriate was not
that understood by the king who found it particularly difficult to
appreciate the legitimacy of opposition. His failure to learn
English and his obvious preference for Hanover further contributed to this sense of alien rule, causing complaint, among Whigs
as well as Tories. In 1718, Friedrich Bonet, the Prussian envoy,
reported that George disliked Britain for its language, constitution, political parties and continual importunities for royal favour,
whereas he was master of all of those in Hanover.

Bonet also noted that, in contrast, the Prince and Princess of
Wales, then linked to the opposition, conspicuously always spoke
English. Public from 1717, this rift began a series of disagree-
ments between Hanoverian kings and their heirs. Thus, in 1737,
George II informed diplomats in London, via his Minister of the
Ceremonies, Sir Clermont Cotterell, that it was his wish that they
should not go to the court of Frederick, Prince of Wales, and
subsequent instructions to envoys took note of these views.

Concern about George I's goals was exacerbated by a sense
that his preference for Hanover entailed an abandonment of
British national interests, as resources were expended for the
aggrandisement of Hanover, and as the entire direction of foreign

policy was set accordingly. Jacobite propaganda made much of the Germanic nature of the Hanoverian regime. Furthermore, William III had been both son and husband to Stuart princesses and was careful not to proscribe the Tories, but George was easier to attack. If individual Tories were accommodated, it was only at the price of abandoning their colleagues and principles. After George came to the throne in 1714, Tories were dismissed from most posts, in large part because of the alleged sympathy of many with Jacobitism, while parliamentary business was also resolutely partisan. In 1721, Thomas, Duke of Newcastle, a rising Whig, was told by George that he was 'determined to stand by the Whigs'. By turning against the Tories, George encouraged their support for Jacobitism, but the rising of 1715–16 in Scotland and northern England was suppressed, as was a smaller-scale Spanish-backed rising in Scotland in 1719.

Dynastic Rivalry

'That, Gentlemen, is the short and long of the dispute, are you for King George, or the Pretender.'

The anonymous 1747 election broadsheet
To the Worthy Freemen of the City of York

On the other hand, rather than any wholesale Hanoverian take-over, the situation was more like the dual monarchy of nineteenth-century Austria-Hungary. George adapted to British institutions, conforming to the Church of England, despite his strong Lutheranism. Unlike James II and 'James III', George was a pragmatist who was sensible enough to adapt and survive. Lacking the decisiveness, charisma and wiliness of Louis XIV and Peter the Great, George did not have an impact or win a reputation comparable to either, but their ambitions, and notably the transformative plans of the latter, were out of keeping with his position.

Differences with his son George over position and patronage led to a full-scale breakdown in relations in 1717, one linked to division within the government. 1720 brought reconciliations of a sort, although there was still the need to overcome the financial scandal of the South Sea Company in 1720 and to thwart the Jacobite Atterbury Plot in 1722. In his last years, George showed both political skills and a sense of responsibility. He was no incompetent and unyielding monarch threatening the end of Hanoverian rule in Britain. George also remained active, indeed the most active in his last years of all the Hanoverian monarchs. The ministerial correspondence covering George's visit to Hanover in 1725 shows the king playing an active role in scrutinising documents and mediating governmental decisions. George's visits to Hanover in 1723 and 1725 also saw bouts of diplomatic activity in which he played a major role.

A warrior against the French in the 1670s, 1690s and 1700s, and the Turks in 1683–5, George was far from being a militaristic dolt. He had cultural and intellectual interests, including an active engagement with the scientific research of the Royal Society, and was keen to have his granddaughters inoculated against small-pox. He also planned the university at Göttingen, something brought to fruition during the reign of his son, and, in 1724, founded the Regius Professorships in Modern History at the Universities of Cambridge and Oxford.

George's reputation as a supporter of toleration, seen in his attempt to ease the position of Dissenters, can be related to enlightened ideas as well as to prudential political considerations, since they tended to vote Whig, and encouraged Voltaire to dedicate his *Henriade* to him. When Voltaire took refuge in Britain, he was helped by George.

A keen supporter of Italian opera in London and a patron of George Frideric Handel, George also liked concerts and masquerades. Interested in building, he was responsible for extensive work on Kensington Palace, including the completion and decoration of new state rooms and the remodelling of the grounds, where he liked to take long evening walks.

After having initially pursued a very divisive foreign policy, and accordingly coming to support ministers with divisive domestic views, George eventually helped to make the political system work effectively, bringing a valuable measure of political stability.

Discussing Royal Power

'... though the People's sense may not be the Prince's rule directing or imposing; it may notwithstanding be his reason moving and persuading; nor is it below the majesty of a prince to take his measures sometimes from this rise, and in some measure guiding his resolutions and councils thereby. The wisest of princes in past ages have done so; and acted accordingly.'

Daniel Defoe, *Reasons for a War* (1729)

GEORGE II

The succession of George II (1727–60) was peaceful, although in 1745 he was to face the most serious crisis of any for the Hanoverian dynasty, when Jacobite forces under Charles Edward Stuart (Bonnie Prince Charlie) advanced toward London as far as Derby. The subsequent battle of Culloden in 1746 was very much a dynastic clash, reminiscent in many respects of the Wars of the Roses. Charles Edward Stuart, the elder grandson of James II and VII, was defeated by William, Duke of Cumberland, the younger son of George.

Much of George's energy was directed to politics where the king repeatedly felt boxed in. Having failed to prevent the fall of the Walpole ministry in 1742, George did not want to turn to the Tories to support the ministry and, instead, wished to employ favourites such as John Lord Carteret. Yet he also regarded as essential the 'Old Corps' Whigs, those who had wielded power

---

Verses for Royalty

Poet Laureates were, and still are, expected to praise royals. Nahum Tate wielded his pen from 1692 until 1715 across changes in monarch. His verses for George I's birthday in 1715 included reference to the succession in the shape of George, Prince of Wales and his wife Caroline:

> Yet long before our royal sun,
> His destined course has run,
> We are blessed to see a glorious heir,
> That shall the mighty loss repair,
> When he that blazes now, shall this low sphere resign,
> In a sublimer orb eternally to shine.

> A Cynthia too, adorned with every grace
> Of person and of mind,
> And happy in a starry race,
> Of such auspicious kind,
> As joyfully presage,
> No want of royal heirs, in any future age.

---

under Walpole, who were implacably opposed to those favourites. He responded with his characteristic mixture of pragmatism and choleric anger.

Keen on military matters and enjoying the company of military men, George participated in the battle of Oudenaarde in 1708, charging the French at the head of the Hanoverian dragoons, and having his horse shot from under him, an episode that was to be referred to frequently. He commanded against the French at Dettingen in 1743. The monarchs sought to ensure professionalism in the military, emphasising competence rather than connections. Thanks to their personal experience, George I and George II were particularly adept at doing so. Visits to Hanover in 1729, 1732, 1735,

1736, 1741, 1743, 1745, 1748, 1750, 1752 and 1755 provided George with opportunities to review troops and to hunt.

George matched his father in arguing with his eldest son, Frederick, Prince of Wales, who would have become king had George lived for only as long as his father had done. They had particularly poisonous relations from 1737 and Frederick's support for the opposition in the 1741 general election helped cause Walpole's fall. Frederick then became more accommodating, only to oppose the ministry anew, both in the 1747 election and until his death in 1751. In contrast to George's long life, the king's vivacious and highly intelligent wife, Princess Caroline of Ansbach, also born in 1683, died in 1737. George then settled down into a domestic relationship with his already-established mistress, Amalia Sophie Marianne von Wallmoden, whom he had met in Hanover. After Caroline died, George made her Countess of Yarmouth, and her role became similar to that of Melusine von der Schulenburg under his father. She became an influential political force while giving George a welcome harmony.

The private tributes paid to George when he died are striking, especially as it might not have been thought that the cantankerous monarch would have inspired such respect and affection. The 'bluestocking' Elizabeth Montagu offered a very personal assessment:

> With him our laws and liberties were safe, he possessed in a great degree, the confidence of his people and the respect of foreign governments; and a certain steadiness of character made him of great consequence in these unsettled times. During his long reign we never were subject to the insolence and rapaciousness of favourites, a grievance of all others most intolerable ... His character would not afford subject for epic poetry, but will look well in the sober page of history. Conscious perhaps of this, he was too little regardful of sciences and the fine arts; he considered common sense as his best panegyric.

Most turned to the bright promise of a new, young and vigorous king, in the person of his grandson, George III, leaving Sarah Stanley to note six weeks later:

> I cannot help regretting our late sovereign. If he had some defects, he had certainly many virtues, and he had experience, which nothing but time can give; yet he seems already to be almost forgotten.

'Frederick I'

As a patron, George's eldest son, Frederick, Prince of Wales (1707–51), was much more important: he was a significant supporter of music, literature and landscape gardening, and an important and discerning patron of the Rococo style. Frederick was painted in 1733 by Philip Mercier, playing music with his sisters Anne and Caroline, while another sister, Amelia, listened with a volume of Milton in her lap: he indeed played the bass viol and, as shown in the painting, the cello. From the mid-1730s, Frederick took an active political role in opposition to his father and the latter's support for the Walpole ministry. This included the prince's patronage of the Lincoln's Inn Fields theatre as a rival to George II's theatrical politics. Frederick displayed his 'rebellion' by supporting (according to some, co-writing) opposition plays put on in this theatre. Thus, theatre was as much charged with Hanoverian dynastic politics as with Hanoverian politics. The recipients of Frederick's patronage included the Anglo-Scot James Thomson, who received an annual pension of £100 and contributed to the Masque *Alfred* (1740), providing the words for 'Rule Britannia'. *Alfred*, which David Mallet wrote jointly with Thomson. This was not alone among the literature of exalted patriotism inspired by Frederick's opposition to the Walpole ministry. In *Alfred*, the hermit predicted:

the virtue,
> The great, the glorious passions that will fire
> Distant posterity when guardian laws
> Are by the patriot, in the glowing senate,
> Won from corruption.

This represented a very different role from that earlier taken by Frederick, whose active love life had been the subject of James Miller's *Vanelia: or The Amours of the Great* (1732), the text of an unperformed opera that went through at least six editions. The hunting of animals by Frederick was the subject of group pictures by John Wootton in 1729 and 1734. Frederick was also seen as a supporter for the creation of an academy for the arts, a project brought to fruition under his son and successor, George III.

GEORGE III

Becoming king at the age of twenty-two in 1760, as a result of succeeding his grandfather, George III (1760–1820) was the youngest in that position since Edward VI, who had been a child. This youth proved very important to the determined way in which he took up the charge, as did the education he had received and his reaction against his grandfather.

George's names, George William Frederick, proclaimed his impeccable dynastic and Whig credentials, but were no security for a child born two months premature in 1738. There were doubts that the prince would survive, and indeed many had not over previous centuries, but Mary Smith, one of the key figures who so easily slip from public attention, proved an effective wet-nurse. Characteristically, George showed gratitude, appointing Mary his laundress when king and having her youngest daughter succeed her.

As with other heirs, George was educated to kingship, but in his case this did not focus on military matters. Instead, he concentrated on the political beliefs of his father, Frederick, Prince of Wales, who was committed to the idea of a 'Patriot King', a monarch who could rise above party interests, and notably the very clear commitment of George I and George II to the Whigs. Based on the arguments of Henry, Viscount Bolingbroke, a one-time Tory, who had, from the 1720s, sought to articulate a 'Country' opposition to the governing Whigs, this idea focused assumptions about the proper character of kingship. In particular, the 'Patriot King' was seen as a national redeemer, a unifying figure. This idea was to be very important to the development of British kingship. It linked traditional ideas to the modern practice of monarchy, and, like both, brought together both religious and secular concepts, each having a powerful component of justice.

George's constitutionalism, however, was to be confused by the realities of politics, which were made more pressing by his naivety, for Frederick's early death meant that George would not face the opportunities of coming to the throne after experience of life. Also there had been no earlier experience under a Frederick I in bedding down the concept of a 'Patriot King'.

A related aspect of George's upbringing and his determination to improve the country was provided by his strong religious commitment, which represented a return to the clear piety and devotion of Queen Anne and looked forward to those of Elizabeth II. This commitment is apt to be downplayed in a secular age, both in commentary and in history, but it was fundamental to George's life, character and policies. Contemporaries noted the energy with which he said his amens. George I and George II might have been Supreme Governors of the Church of England and in communion with the Church, dutifully attending Anglican worship, but they were Lutherans by upbringing and practice. Although not especially devout, they were observant. An Anglican from the outset, George took his piety into his politics, with the idea of service and commitment being important to both. However, this drive meant that he repeatedly found it difficult to excuse, or understand, let alone sympathise with, those who held different views or followed other lifestyles. His Christian convictions were very much framed in terms of duty. A sense of struggle played a role in his self-identity and shaped his assessment of other people. Those who struggled to command themselves and prevail over temptation earned his respect, while others who surrendered he distrusted.

George thought it necessary that, once he became king, he should take a central political role, which he saw not only as his constitutional responsibility but also as his moral duty. As king, George's timetable and correspondence denoted effort, his handwritten letters dated to the second he started writing them, which also reflected his interest in timepieces. A young man with expectations of change became a young king in a hurry to transform the situation. He found reality, in the shape of the critical and/or unwilling responses of others, as well as his own limitations, repeatedly galling in the 1760s, but he learned to cope and played a major role in creating a new ministerial pattern that brought stability in the early 1770s under Frederick, Lord North, First Lord of the Treasury from 1770 to 1782. Reality, in the same shape, then brought an unexpected total breakdown in America in 1775 and, eventually, a near political collapse in Britain in 1782-4. There was again a fresh start through a new ministerial system which had both the strength to bring stability in the peace years that ended in 1763, and the resilience thereafter that proved crucial in the face of repeated failures and problems in dealing with revolutionary pressures, internal and external.

For George, there was pleasure in each of these periods of success, but much anger and some soul-searching in those of failure. Despite his great popularity on his accession and at his coronation, George soon became a figure of controversy because of his determination to reign without party. As a result, the theme of the king as a dangerous political force exerting a malevolent role in British affairs, one long deployed by opponents of particular monarchs, was to be strongly revived in the 1760s.

In the meanwhile, George got married as monarch, a situation that had not occurred since Charles II. The maintenance of the dynasty was a key aspect of kingship, and in George's case the sources permit an unprecedented understanding of the factors involved. In 1759, when he was twenty-one, George fell in love with Lady Sarah Lennox, a beautiful fifteen-year-old who was the sister of Charles, 3rd Duke of Richmond (later Master-General of the Ordnance under George) and sister-in-law of Henry Fox. George, however, realised that this was unlikely to be an acceptable match, both because she was a commoner (and thus unacceptable as Electress of Hanover) and because Fox was a highly controversial politician, and accepted the advice of his confidant, John, 3rd Earl of Bute, not to pursue the matter. Yet, despite George's belief that only marriage would end the struggle between prudence and his desire for a woman, he was unwilling, while still a prince, to seek a German princess, which reflected his view that any such negotiation would give too much of an opportunity for George II to intervene.

Once king, George sought a German Protestant princess. The criteria he employed centred on disposition and child-bearing ability. A Catholic bride from a royal house, the choice of Charles I and Charles II, was no longer politically possible in Britain. Factors for exclusion among those princesses initially considered included being too young, or, having socially questionable marriages among ancestors, and being bad-tempered, or inclined to secularism, or unlikely to have children. Charlotte of Mecklenburg-Strelitz was eventually left alone in the field, and the difficulty of her being a Lutheran was ended when she expressed her readiness to conform to the Church of England. Allegedly a descendant of Afonso III of Portugal and his African mistress, Charlotte had been called the first modern mixed-race royal, but there is no reliable evidence for this claim.

With his irritable personality and emphasis on duty, George certainly could not have always been a relaxing spouse. Yet, the couple had similar views, spent a lot of time together and had a successful marriage, certainly at least until the consequences of George's poor health hit hard after 1801. They had a sexually active marriage, at least judged by the fifteen children they produced. There were plentiful signs of affection, as on George's return from Portsmouth in 1773:

> When he came to Kew he was so impatient to see the Queen that he opened the chaise himself and jumped out before any of his attendants could come to his assistance. He seized the Queen, whom he met at the door, round the waist, and carried her in his arms into the room.

Marriage gave George a stability and comfort he was not to find with all his children; and with, on the whole, a calmness that differed from the histrionics that later marked Victoria's response to Prince Albert.

George's personality can also be readily followed in his correspondence. Written by George himself, it was more copious than that of any predecessor, and whereas, to a degree, they are figures known from the outside, with George there is the repeatedly expressed interior view. Prone to see matters in black and white, he displayed a generally cool nerve in confrontations, total conviction of rectitude, and a bloody-minded determination to have his way that followed from the assumption that he alone was taking a principled stand. His tone of moral superiority and inflexibility often offended. A naïve idealist, George valued integrity and fidelity, but did not appreciate the nuances of politics and government, nuances defined and defended by self-serving politicians who were not easy to deal with. His moral reformism, which drew on his strong personal piety, was specifically aimed against what he saw as faction and luxury. In the 1780s, George was to support the Proclamation Society (which became the Society for the Suppression of Vice) and the various moral reform societies.

However, by the late 1760s, George had focused on the narrower task of charting a path between political factions to create a ministry with which he could be comfortable. Growing problems in the management of the American colonies helped derail this process, but not his monarchical personality. He retained throughout both conscientiousness and a conviction that personal merit was crucial to appointment, promotion and conduct in both Church and state. His reluctance to award unmerited patronage extended even to his family.

As a young man, George III followed his father, Frederick, Prince of Wales, in neither being trained for war, nor being given opportunities to serve, despite his firmly pressed request to do so in 1759, which was rejected by George II. George III, nevertheless, took an interest in military matters, as well as fulfilling his responsibilities. His determination to increase effectiveness involved not only reviews and the oversight of promotions, but also consideration of weaponry. In 1786, Sir William Fawcett, the Adjutant General, returned to George two guns the king had sent him, 'the bayonet of that which is intended for the Light Infantry having been made to fix, agreeably to your Majesty's directions'.

Increasingly, George had more knowledge and experience than some of his ministers. In 1771, he told Sir Stanier Porten, an under-secretary, of his conviction that government offices must ensure: 'regularity and secrecy . . . clearness essentially necessary. System and secrecy the fundamentals of offices. Disliked circulation [of papers], believed few read papers themselves, at least few could enter into discourse with him on any matter.' Having had a ninety-minute audience on his return in 1787 from northern Europe, Sir John Sinclair 'was astonished with the extent of information which the King displayed upon a variety of subjects'. In

1793, reading 'with great attention' a draft declaration to the French nation by William Grenville, the Foreign Secretary, George corrected both the copyist and the original.

Conscientiousness and the sense of responsibility that the king strove to inculcate in his children can be related not only to George's piety and sense of morality, but also to his mental health. No simple explanation is satisfactory: George's desire for order may have owed something to his personality, or even to his concern about his own irritable anxiety when faced by disorder, but his beliefs about his role are also pertinent. An emphasis on order certainly affected George's relations with his family, not least with his three brothers who were very different from George in personality and behaviour, notably Henry, Duke of Cumberland (1745–90); this underlines the need not to place too great an emphasis on clashes between the generations. In 1770, George had to lend Cumberland the money he owed as a result of an affair with Harriet, Lady Grosvenor, and in 1771 the duke had a clandestine marriage with a commoner. The furious George, who failed to get Cumberland to disavow the marriage, barred him from his presence, and actively sponsored the Royal Marriages Act of 1772 which gave the king a position of legal authority over his family's marriages, an issue that affected his relations with his children. The minority of peers who opposed the legislation presented it as an infringement of constitutional values.

Under the Act, descendants of George II, with the exception of the descendants of princesses who married abroad, could only marry before the age of twenty-five with royal permission. Thereafter, they had to give a year's notice to the Privy Council, and Parliament had not to expressly disapprove of the marriage. George, Prince of Wales's secret marriage of 1785 to Maria Fitzherbert was in defiance of this Act, as well as of the 1701 Act of Settlement because she was a Catholic. When he was informed that a favourite son, Augustus, had married the pregnant Lady Augusta Murray in 1793, George ordered the government to proceed in accordance with the Royal Marriages Act, and the marriage was declared void the following year. Meanwhile, Cumberland as well as another of George's brothers, William, Duke of Gloucester, who had also married secretly, had not been received at Court until 1780 when the offer of help in the Gordon Riots changed the king's attitude; even thereafter, their wives were never received.

Meanwhile, in his artistic patronage, George had moved from his earlier focus on Italianate work, on the purchase of which he had spent heavily in 1762–3, to add more classical and national themes. His admiration for Poussin and the classical inheritance led him to commission 'history works', moral accounts of classical episodes, including *Timon of Athens* from Nathaniel Dance in 1765 and *The Departure of Regulus* from Benjamin West in 1768, which was a widespread artistic preference of the period, reflecting the notion that culture should be exemplary: Timon rejected luxury and Regulus was a self-sacrificing hero of Republican Rome. Culture was linked to patriotism in the foundation of the Royal Academy in 1768, which George helped finance, and which he honoured by knighting the President, Joshua Reynolds, in 1769. George was also a key patron of Thomas Gainsborough from whom he commissioned a series of portraits of the royal family, which was artistically bold, as Gainsborough's sparing use of paint was less fashionable than Reynolds's habit of slapping it on. George, who was called 'a good connoisseur' by Gainsborough, also favoured Paul Sandby, a master of the watercolour, and West, whom he appointed Historical Painter to the king in 1772 and to whom he gave much patronage, notably at Windsor Castle.

George took a keen interest in the theatre, both in London and on his tours, and was fond of music. He played the flute, harpsichord (frequently), and pianoforte, and collected music, including works by Lully, Palestrina and Scarlatti. He also actively collected copies and arrangements of Handel's oratorios in the 1760s, and, in the early 1770s, was presented by Handel's amanuensis, John Smith, with the composer's manuscript scores and harpsichord. In the 1780s, he patronised the revival of Handel oratorios – with their religious themes – but not the operas.

Spending a lot of money on his library, George was particularly interested in books on theology, history, jurisprudence, science, the arts, and the classical inheritance; less so in fiction. He opened his library to interested readers. Meeting Samuel Johnson in 1767, the king was able to discuss books of sermons with him, George praising seventeenth-century writers such as Robert Sanderson, a chaplain to and a favourite preacher before Charles I, who lost his living and the divinity chair at Oxford because he refused to subscribe to the Parliamentarians' Solemn League and Covenant. Johnson both advised on the purchase of books for the royal family and was a beneficiary of the largesse of the king who also appointed the prominent historian William Robertson Historiographer Royal in Scotland.

George was deeply interested in the past, and, to a degree, reverential of it, while he was reflective when he visited the tomb of the overthrown and murdered Edward II in Gloucester Cathedral in 1788. When his brother Henry married a commoner in 1771, the outraged and overwrought George informed another brother, William, that such a step might threaten civil war, as he claimed that the fifteenth-century Wars of the Roses owed much to the intermarriage of Crown and nobility. George also took a clear view on legitimacy that made allowance for the cause of the Stuarts, an allowance that extended from 1799 to providing financial support for 'Henry IX', the younger son of 'James III', who succeeded on the death of Charles Edward (Bonnie Prince Charlie) in 1788 to the Jacobite claim but was a Cardinal and therefore not in a position to pass on the claim. George had no time for the false report that 'James III', the 'Warming Pan Baby' of 1688, was a changeling.

In 1799, an overture on behalf of Henry IX, whose property had been seized by the French, led George to reflect that he had 'ever thought that the true solid basis' of Hanoverian rule was that 'it came to preserve the free constitution of this empire, both in church and state, which compact I trust none of my successors will ever dare to depart from'.

George was mindful of what the Glorious Revolution meant in terms of the rejection of unacceptable monarchy. In his writings as a prince, George criticised James II, arguing that the Glorious Revolution had rescued Britain 'from the iron rod of arbitrary power', and praised Oliver Cromwell as 'a friend of justice and virtue', while, separately, distinguishing those in the opposition to Charles I 'who, not content with removing abuses, were for removing foundations'.

George saw his position and that of future British monarchs as resting, not solely on dynastic right, but on duty. In 1764, Parliament resolved that Timothy Brecknock's *Droit Le Roy, Or a Digest of the Rights and Prerogatives of the Imperial Crown of Great Britain* was 'Jacobitical and violating the Bill of Rights and the Revolution' of 1688–9 and it was burned.

Like his father, George, who had been taught physics and chemistry as a boy, was interested in science. Naturally inquisitive, and displaying an eclectic intelligence which had the insight to appreciate the ideas of those he recognised as more learned than himself, George revived royal links with the Royal Society, and collected scientific instruments. Princess Augusta showed how well she knew her son when she had William Chambers design the King's Observatory as a gift to enable him to watch the transit of Venus in 1769. When he visited Oxford in 1785, George went to the observatory there. Always interested in how things were made, and in making them himself, George, after touring Portsmouth in 1773, pressed for details on how ropes were made for the navy.

George's engagement with watches, clocks, astronomy, botany, and the music of Handel, has been attributed to a striving to take refuge from the pressures of his personality in obsessive intellectual activities centring on the clear demonstration of order and regularity. This is argument by assertion, and reductive, ignoring in particular the role of individual interest and general fashion. Astronomy, botany, and the accurate measurement of time and longitude, were all beneficiaries of the latter, and many who shared in this interest presumably did not share George's psychological profile. Was George's zest for hunting a desire to escape the travails of his life, a preference for open air pursuits, the product of a frustrated desire to command, a substitute for military activity, or something else? George's interest in things mechanical far predated the political pressures of his succession as king. Louis XVI shared George's interest in hunting, botany, watches and clocks, but had a very different personality.

As far as the arts and sciences are concerned, it is best to note George's role not as a spectator but as an informed and committed patron, with wide-ranging cultural and intellectual interests and a desire to become engaged, as he showed in his performance of music. He made available the royal apartments in Somerset House for the Royal Academy from 1771, and, although, like most monarchs, he is not usually regarded as an intellectual, George was interested in the arts and sciences in a way that his two predecessors were not.

Fundamental to his perception of kingship, George was an active supporter of the Church of England, with a strong faith, unlike his father, grandfather and great-grandfather. The promise of 'endless bliss' after death was real to the king, as was gratitude to the 'Great Preserver', ever-present and watchful. George's dependence for salvation on divine mercy, not on human merit, was accompanied by a belief in the need to show thanks for the divine gift of life by means of appropriate conduct. These beliefs guided George's conduct and helped structure his time. Sundays were special to him and he tried not to handle government business then, while Court life deferred to religious duty, and no levees, drawing rooms or card-playing were held during Passion or Whit weeks. George repeatedly saw divine intervention at work in the affairs of man, and awareness of God and divine injunctions as being a particular guide to monarchs, and, linked to that, a duty and a responsibility.

George made religious issues even more central in politics than they might otherwise have been, and helped ensure that those of the Anglican devout, mostly Tories, who had been uneasy about the Glorious Revolution and the Hanoverian Succession rallied to the Crown, strengthening the identity both of the Church of England and of the nation, which matched (and was linked to) the political reconciliation with the Tories. This reconciliation was of help in sustaining the difficult, long, and costly struggle with American 'Patriots' (rebels), but could not bring success. Indeed, the strains of the war undid George's political achievement and forced him in 1782 to accept successive ministries he distrusted. The resulting political crisis was one in which George emerged triumphant in 1784, rather as Charles II had done from the Exclusion Crisis in 1681, but it placed George under great personal strain and led, amid some histrionic language, to a threat to abdicate.

At the same time, George had an opportunity to show the leadership in adversity that he was subsequently to display during the French Revolutionary War. He associated himself closely with the war effort, not only in his correspondence with ministers but also in public displays. These included visiting the fleet at Chatham and Portsmouth and touring military encampments as France and Spain launched an invasion plan. There was no memorable speech comparable to that given by Elizabeth I at Tilbury in 1588 in response to the Spanish Armada, but there was a similar sense of nationhood focused on the king. In 1780, the exhibition at the Royal Academy displayed West's *Portrait of His Majesty* (1779), showing George in military uniform and holding a document.

In 1780, George faced a very difficult challenge in the shape of the Gordon Riots in London, which arose because of anger about measures to ease the legal position for Catholics. In the ensuing violence, George pressed for resolution, and, whereas the magistrates panicked and refused to act, the unflustered king remained firm. 'Convinced till the magistrates have ordered some military execution on the rioters this town will not be restored to order,' George summoned the Privy Council which empowered the army to employ force without the prior permission of a magistrate. George was then instrumental in the deployment and use of the troops that ended the crisis.

George's sense of order was challenged not only by politics, but also by his family. Whereas the difficulties he had encountered with his siblings had made George more acutely concerned about his children, the outcome was no happier, and, as their numerous children grew to adulthood, a conflict arose between George and Charlotte's sense of propriety and the dissolute life adopted by most of their brood of boys. In 1780, George had urged Frederick, Duke of York, to read the Bible every morning and evening, not least because it provided the opportunity for self-examination. The members of the younger generation were especially loath to accept the king and queen's views on marriage and choice of marriage partners, and entered into liaisons which, while often stable and personally fulfilling, hardly lived up to the increasingly respectable, almost prudish, image that George wished to promote. The alienation between the generations was represented most strikingly in the endless disputes between George and the Prince of Wales. One scandal succeeded another. In 1781, George had to pay £5,000 to buy back the love letters that the prince had written his mistress, Mary Robinson, a prominent actress whom he had seen playing Perdita. Irrespective of the problem of the heir, the need for establishments for his sons was a financial strain for George.

These were difficult years for George in other ways. He had had no experience of miscarriages or stillborn infants to prepare him for the grief when the first of his children died. Born in 1780,

Alfred died in 1782, followed in 1783 by Octavius, who had been born in 1779. God was certainly testing George in his family as well as his reign. George was a very domestic monarch, which was an outcome of his character and interests. Indeed, the fluidity of unconstrained public socialising clearly worried the king and separated him from his sons. His hostility to masquerades was indicative of his sustained preference for integrity over artificiality and performance. This critique of affectation was both an aesthetic and a moral choice, and his increased dislike of London and favour for the country was another aspect of it. George also thought early nights a good idea, and rose early. A dislike of show, and a concern to avoid the consequences of overeating and drunkenness, contributed, alongside his shyness and parsimony, to a simple lifestyle. This way of life, which accorded with the strengthening of the ideals of privacy and family life in the French and Habsburg Courts, alongside his interest in and pursuit of farming, was to lead to the king being known as 'Farmer George', with its suggestion of ordinariness and accessibility as well as patriotism.

The Court struck observers as pleasantly domestic or dull, and certainly the opposite of grand. George generally wore simple clothes, including on his birthday, but wore new clothes for Charlotte's. In the midst of frequently splendid entertainment, he was cautious in what he ate and drank, trying not to eat sugar and drinking little, and was a model of slimness compared with his eldest son. His hostile attitude to sugar was based on health and not the role of slaves. Preferring family meals to banquets, and avoiding grandness, both in what he ate and in how he was served, George cut down what he ate in the 1790s in response to the domestic crisis caused by poor harvests, thus prefiguring the stance of George V during World War I. Informality was also seen in George moving among his subjects without guards or servants, or with very few. He had a sense of humour and liked to joke, even if his jokes showed affability rather than wit. At Cheltenham, he told the pumper at the spa, Hannah Forty: 'Mrs Forty, you and your husband together make eighty.'

The values of the Court were very different from a world of sexual intrigue. Indeed, somewhat fancifully, a critical French observer reported in 1763 that the Court resembled an affluent bourgeois household with pleasures constrained by matrimony. Well aware that 'little attentions often do good', George made a practice of speaking to all who attended his levées, which brought him in touch with most of the social élite and indeed with many individuals whom he did not know or did not know well. This was a strain for George and for those he met, as, under Court etiquette, which continues to this day, George had to speak first, and courtesy required him to press on if those he met were too nervous to say anything, or if they responded with only a few words. A shy child, George learned to speak in public and to put others at their ease, and those who met the king frequently commented on how agreeable he was, and how much knowledge he showed of individuals and their connections, a characteristic shared with George VI. He was not rude like George II, and was far less waspish than Frederick the Great.

George certainly showed an ease in his contact with people of all ranks that reflected a certainty of position and purpose, and a belief that dignity did not necessarily lie in social distinction. For him, Christian notions of benevolence and human sympathy cut across notions of hierarchy. Nevertheless, George was head of society, as his socialising made clear, while his activities on Court days included the presentations of the young when they came of age, and of brides and bridegrooms to be, which overlapped with more official aspects of the recognition of merit, particularly nominations to peerages, investitures, and the kissing of the king's hand by the newly appointed. George also took an interest in issues of etiquette that arose in high society, and his role as the fount of honour ensured that men and women of rank could expect a private audience if they sought one, providing them with the opportunity to press for patronage.

Ironically, these were the years in which George nearly found lasting fame of a very different type. On 13 March 1781, William Herschel, Hanoverian-born but British-settled, discovered Uranus, the first planet to be found since antiquity and the first that could not be seen by the naked eye. In honour of the king, Herschel named it the 'Georgium Sidus', a reference to Virgil's *Georgics* that claimed immortality for George. The following year, George met Herschel, who subsequently exhibited his telescope before him and became a pensioner of the Crown.

A shift from the past was not always easy to accept, as with contrasting American evaluations of George in the mid-1780s.

> I saw, at once, that the ulcerations in the narrow mind of that mulish being left nothing to be expected on the subject of my attendance.

In his autobiography, written thirty-five years later, Jefferson thus painted a picture of an ungracious reception from George III of Britain at his *levée* on 17 March 1786. In practice, there are no contemporary accounts of the meeting, and it is likely that Jefferson's description was over-dramatised, if not totally misleading. Linked to this response was the fact that Jefferson mistakenly blamed his failure to negotiate a trade treaty on George, which exaggerated the latter's role in commercial diplomacy.

A very different impression, that of wise and honest courtesy, was made when George received John Adams on 1 June 1785 as the first American minister to the Court of St James. Adams recorded George as saying:

> I have done nothing in the late contest [the War of American Independence, 1775–83] but what I thought myself indispensably bound to do, by the duty which I

owed to my people . . . I was the last to consent to the separation; but the separation having been made, and having become inevitable, I have always said, as I say now, that I would be the first to meet the friendship of the United States as an independent power . . . let the circumstances of language, religion, and blood have their natural and full effect.

George, who, Adams noted, was 'much affected, and answered me with more tremor than I had spoken with', was revealed as informed and relaxed. With 'an air of familiarity, and smiling, or rather laughing', he astutely teased Adams by saying 'there is an opinion among some people that you are not the most attached of all your countrymen to the manners of France'. The wrong-footed Adams stood on his dignity. 'Surprised' and 'embarrassed', he responded that he had 'no attachment but to my own country'; which George, 'as quick as lightning', courteously trumped, saying 'an honest man will never have any other'.

The extent to which George's serious illness in 1788–9 contributed to a major political crisis was strong evidence of his continued political, constitutional and symbolic importance, for his symptoms of insanity precipitated the Regency Crisis. George's health had generally been good, but, in late October 1788, possibly as a result of bipolar disorder, he began to talk rapidly and uncontrollably, becoming delirious in early November. At the time of the attack, George was fifty, and the auguries for a long life were not good, as his father had died at the age of forty-four, and of George's eight siblings, six died before the age of fifty. The alternation of apparent madness with intervals of lucidity, of paroxysms of rage with hours of calm, proved particularly disconcerting, and not only to others for, when lucid, George was aware of his situation.

It was clear that if there was to be a regency, George, Prince of Wales, now of age, would be regent. The ministry would therefore change, as the prince was close, politically and personally, to Charles James Fox, the opposition leader. The extent of his likely powers as regent, however, was unclear, and the political interest and inherent drama of the occasion attracted intense public interest. The conduct of the prince and of the Whigs, who were eager for power and hopeful of George's death or continued madness, aroused much criticism, which, in turn, greatly encouraged sympathy for George.

George's summer travels after his recovery in 1789 drew even larger crowds than those in 1788, and, alongside growing signs of division in France, this burst of royal popularity generated confidence in the British system, marking a major change in attitude from the early 1780s. There was a rallying of the social élite and of much opinion around Country, Crown and Church, that prefigured the loyalism of the 1790s in opposition to the French Revolution and the attendant radicalism in Britain.

Seeking to strengthen his recovery, 1789 saw George's first visit to Weymouth, where he found the sea air and bathing 'certainly agrees'. The king's trip there gave a new significance to his travels, but also confirmed his already-established tendency to visit only southern England. He visited Weymouth every year bar three from 1789 to 1805, but never Liverpool, Manchester, Leeds, York, Newcastle or Norwich, let alone Hanover, Ireland, Scotland and Wales. Whereas George I had taken the waters at Pyrmont in Germany, George III took those at Cheltenham. He also toured industrial sites, including a pin manufactory at Gloucester, a carpet works and a china factory at Worcester, the carpet works at Axminster, and the canals and cloth industry near Stroud.

Visiting Worcester in 1788 for the Three Choirs Festival in the cathedral, George added his own private band to the orchestra. The festival brought together many of George's concerns, as it was intended for the relief of the widows and orphans of the clergy and included a cathedral service, and his visit provided him with an opportunity to display royal bounty: he left ten guineas for the workmen at the china factory he visited, £50 for the poor of the city (with another £50 from the queen), £200 for the clergy widows and orphans, £300 to liberate debtors, and his pardon to deserving criminals awaiting transportation. The king thus demonstrated concern about the moral and physical welfare of all, which, alongside Christian charity and care for others, was important to the extent and motivation of his philanthropy and a counterpart to celebrating the nation's triumphs. George's stance looked forward toward the later emphasis in the royal family on charitable philanthropy.

In response to the French Revolution, George was not an ultra. However, he was correctly wary of claims about the scale of royalist support in France, and did not press for the restoration of the Bourbons as a crucial war goal, yet, although unenthusiastic about fighting on for them, he came to agree that Jacobinism could not be destroyed 'unless Royalty is re-established'. George wanted France beaten, and, whether Britain experienced victory or defeat in the war, he pressed for resolve in the struggle. In James Gillray's 1793 caricature 'A new Map of England and France. The French Invasion; or John Bull bombarding the Bum-Boats', in which the French threat is dispersed with excremental force, John Bull was given George's face.

George kept a close eye on military policy and made informed comments. Unlike most of the leading ministers of the period, the king had had experience in directing a war, that of American Independence, although this was not successful.

King and ministry united in pursuit of victory, but there were tensions. Facing France's military successes from 1794, the ministry, much to George's concern, was more willing than he was to begin negotiations with Paris. George doubted that a lasting peace could be negotiated with an outlaw regime that lacked legitimacy and he believed that France had to be defeated before there could be a basis for fruitful negotiations, an attitude that adversely affected his response to negotiations in 1796 and 1797. In addition, he characteristically adopted a moral tone, and feared that seeking peace would weaken Britain accordingly: for George, the issue of negotiations was one in which honour and integrity were both to the fore and aspects of prudence. The failure of negotiations in 1797, which eased tensions with the ministry, left George hopeful that, if Britain acted firmly, it could win an honourable and lasting peace, helped by factional struggles in Paris and the exhaustion of French resources. He read Edmund Burke's *Reflections* and said that every gentleman should read it.

However, over Catholic Emancipation, he was unwilling to match the government and brought up his coronation oath to protect the established church and the confessional state. In his case, inherent conservatism was linked to a stubborn determination to protect the constitution and the Church of England, and, thus, the traditional, as well as legal, character of authority and power.

George's dispute with William Pitt the Younger, First Lord of the Treasury from 1783 to 1801 and 1804 to 1806, over this issue was not to the fore as far as the public was concerned. Instead, the monarchy had become a potent symbol of national identity and continuity in response to the French Revolution. George benefited from the strength not only of loyalism, in the sense of an active opposition to democratic and republican tendencies, but also of loyal adherence to non-partisan principles of constitutional propriety and support for the established order. Opposition criticisms failed to gain political or popular traction. The monarchy played a greater positive role in political ideology than it had done between 1689 and 1746 when it had been compromised by serious differences over the legitimacy of the dynasty, as well as the contentious nature of constitutional arrangements after 1688. But from the 1790s, no such problems hindered a stress on monarchy on the part of conservative elements, and this contributed to the stronger conservative ideology of the period and to the repurposing of monarchy in terms of an active national patriotism, one in which far less critical attention was given to the Hanoverian link.

6

Imperial Majesty

·················

GEORGE III

A chapter break in the midst of a reign, that of George III from 1760 to 1820, can appear a foolish concession to near-century divisions, but in the case of British monarchy under George, such a break captures some important shifts, both public ones and others that are less obvious. For the former, there was the union of the Westminster and Dublin parliaments, the major establishment of British power in India, and the competition with Napoleon, who made himself an emperor in 1804.

For less obvious shifts, there was not only the ageing of George and his more symbolic role, but also the extent to which the greater scale of government, not least, but not only, as a result of the war made the degree of oversight George had attempted earlier no longer feasible. In addition, government became more formal, with the growing role of the Prime Minister and of cabinet methods lessening the significance of individual links between monarch and ministers. The Prime Minister became in effect an office unto itself with its own particular set of responsibilities and was no longer an *ad hoc* addition to being First Lord of the Treasury or another officeholder.

This situation looked toward a major change over the nineteenth century, that of the reduced governmental and political significance of the monarchy. This reduction made it easier for the British empire to have an imperial monarchy of pomp but without the intrusive role that might make the personal responsibilities and views of the monarch difficult and maybe ensure that self-governing colonies followed the North American route. In contrast, imperial monarchy in France was much more a matter of the views and policies of first Napoleon I and later his nephew, Napoleon III (like Louis XVII, Napoleon II did not rule), and was eventually, accordingly, a failure.

The distancing of George from the daily processes of a government expanded to fight with France a war of unprecedented difficulty, a distancing that increasingly characterised the Pitt the Younger years as first minister (1783–1801, 1804–6), also contributed to his growing popularity. This was particularly so as the ministry gained cohesion round Pitt, not least with the grudging dismissal by George in 1792 of Edward, Lord Thurlow, the Lord Chancellor, the last major 'King's Friend'. Unpopular decisions were now blamed on the ministers, while the Crown demonstrated its largely non-partisan usefulness by standing above parties in defence of the constitution, including the constitutionally Established Church, and was thus the guardian of what had become popularly known to its defenders as 'the Protestant constitution'. George himself contributed to this positive image, not by making a special effort to change, but by being himself. In addition, a series of gestures underlined George's commitment to the country. These included the payment of £20,000 from his Privy Purse to the Voluntary Contribution of 1798, and the extension of taxation to the private income of the Crown resulting from the passage of the Crown Private Estates Act of 1800. Yet, alongside this distancing, George continued to take an active interest in government activity, for example that of the navy, visiting Portsmouth after the naval victory at the Glorious First of June in 1794. His was a rulership both active and symbolic.

If in 1742, 1744 and 1782, the British monarchy had appeared one of the weakest in Europe, its rulers unable to sustain in office ministers who enjoyed royal confidence – Walpole, Carteret and North respectively – by 1810, it was the strongest in Europe other than the Romanov regime in Russia, and Napoleon's monarchical dictatorship, which lacked comparable legitimacy. In contrast to the stance of George V toward the Romanovs of Russia once they were overthrown in 1917, under George III other European rulers, such as Louis XVIII of France, the kings of Naples, Portugal and Sardinia, and William V of Orange (first cousin of George), took shelter in Britain, or sought protection behind British forces, especially the navy, as in the cases of Ferdinand IV of Naples in Sicily, Victor Emmanuel I of Savoy-Piedmont in Sardinia, and John VI of Portugal in Brazil.

In this survival and resistance to France, George might appear to be somewhat inconsequential. He had survived bouts of ill-health in 1801 and 1804, but his vigour was fading and his eyesight going; indeed, he was, in some respects, becoming yesterday's man. His political importance, however, was pushed to the fore as a consequence of the revival in the 1800s of minis-terial instability as well as the importance of royal resolve. In his sixties, George was still playing a central role, not least his part in the downfall of Pitt, the most powerful Prime Minister of his reign, in 1801. George's opposition to Catholic Emancipation was crucial in this episode. The establishment of a new ministry in 1801 under Henry Addington, Viscount Sidmouth, a man for whom he had much time, gave George the opportunity to take a more active part in government, which was necessary if a stable ministry was to be created.

Helped by his hostility both to the French Revolution and Napoleon, George remained convinced that politics was a strug-gle of good versus evil, one in which Providence played a key role, but this did not provide an easy basis for policy and politics. Concerned to do the proper thing, George sought to accommo-date change to accustomed order, and, as a consequence, he was opposed to what he saw as unnecessary governmental innova-tion. At the same time, George was a hardworking monarch, and his oversight of government enabled him to make qualitative statements about the conduct of business, as well as to respond to the management of individuals.

The style of monarchy remained public magnificence where necessary, and private modesty, the latter in accordance with 'middle-class' mores and cultural aspirations, and also with that part of the aristocracy adhering to Christian and modest standards. Yet, alongside reports of George as an accessible individual, walking, riding and travelling without pomp and state, indeed any protection (especially outside London), came the reporting of Court life, which presented a very different resonance. Tone and accessibility did not mean that George's lifestyle was that of the middling orders, for he was head of society in what was very much an aristocratic monarchy, making Court routines very important. At the same time, the tone now was very much that of responsible monarchy, not least of the ruler as diligent servant.

George and his family were closely associated with the war effort. On 26 and 28 October 1803, George reviewed 27,000 volunteers in Hyde Park, in each case in front of an estimated half a million people. Through his sons, the royal family played a role in the war effort, notably Frederick, Duke of York, his second son, who was commander-in-chief from 1795 to 1809 and, after a scandal could be overlooked, 1811 to 1827. Although a failed campaign commander in Holland in 1799, York was an effective and impressive administrator, and his care for merit in the army matched his father's for merit in the church. Despite his naval career, the more limited William, Duke of Clarence, his third son, later William IV (1830–7) did not put to sea during the war, but Ernest, Duke of Cumberland, the fifth son, served with Hanoverian forces, gaining a justified reputation for bravery, while Edward, Duke of Kent, the fourth son, a major-general, took part in the capture of Martinique and St Lucia in 1794. The youngest surviving brother, Adolphus, Duke of Cambridge, served as a volunteer with the forces in the Low Countries, but later held command positions, and George's nephew, William, Duke of Gloucester, fought with distinction in the Low Countries.

More generally, the strains that lengthy warfare placed on British society, like its European counterparts, encouraged a looking to symbols of identity. These were particularly significant as nationalism became more important. In the British case, there was no longer a rival dynastic claimant, 'Charles III' having died in obscurity in 1788. Moreover, although the War of American Independence might have left George associated with failure, this was not in fact the case, in part due to his successful emergence from the political crisis of 1782–4. He was fit for the role of symbolic warleader, was needed for this role, and was willing to take it. In turn, George's role helped set the pattern for that of a warleader who was not on the battlefield, even though members of his family would be, a pattern that has continued to the present. Moreover, this role proved very important for the reputation of the monarchy, both in general and with reference to George's reign and its aftermath. In terms of the shifts noted in his reign, there was an important one compounded of the reaction to the Regency Crisis of 1788–9 and, more lastingly, the long-term war from 1793, that produced more popularity for the monarch.

In modern terms, this role against France was less significant than the trans-Atlantic slave trade, which, like the transportation of convicts and the treatment of aboriginal peoples, explains why George's reign has an ambiguous memory across parts of the world, and the anniversaries of claims of territory for the king, under whom James Cook reached Australia, and, later, a British base was established in Botany Bay in 1788, are especially controversial in Australia. The material George retained for his private working library indicates his personal interest in the transoceanic world. It includes Cook's original drawings for the survey of St Pierre and Miquelon islands off Newfoundland, as well as a set of topographical drawings of the new Australian colony. The king financed Cook's first voyage to the Pacific and supported the establishment of botanic gardens at Kew, Calcutta and St Vincent, in order to spread botanical knowledge.

George was happy to approve transportation of felons for life to Botany Bay as a way to build up the new colony. In 1789, he was concerned when three convicted felons chose death instead of transportation: 'It is shocking that men can be so lost to every sentiment of gratitude not to feel the mercy shown them in sparing their lives,' a rejection of a royal act of mercy. They were cajoled into changing their mind. To George, crime represented a defiance of divine guidance that required admonition. This was a heavy duty, and one that he found increasingly difficult to undertake optimistically, noting in 1802 of those who were to be transported: 'as to the reforming the morals of those who have deserved that punishment the King from now a long experience is not sanguine in expectations on that head.' Seriousness, a clear sense of morality, and an awareness of duty, were all clearly present in George's attitude to his role in confirming death sentences. The king was willing to be merciful, responding favourably to recommendations for mercy, but he could also reject them. He believed in the exemplary nature of punishment and was concerned for due process in the shape of maintaining the authority of the judiciary.

After his attack of mania in February 1804, George's health did not return to its previous equilibrium, and he remained easily agitated, leading Pitt that March to avoid meetings likely to upset him. Due to his health, George was unable to attend the spectacular Jubilee fête held in 1809 at Frogmore, only a mile from Windsor. Instead, a portrait of the king was displayed in the temporary temple erected for the occasion. The Jubilee provided a major opportunity for the display of respect and affection for the king as a central part of the patriotism; and celebrations were held across the empire, although there were, unsurprisingly, criticisms of the occasion from radicals.

In 1810, the shock of the fatal illness of his last-born, his favourite daughter Amelia, proved crucial to George's deterioration. It was initially thought that he would be all right despite her illness, but the fact that she did not die quickly helped cause the crisis, and they both declined together. George frequently questioned her doctors on her progress, and was popularly supposed to have been pushed over the edge when Amelia gave him a mourning ring containing a lock of her hair. Symptoms of insanity were obvious by 25 October, the day of his last public appearance.

The ministry moved quickly. On 10 December 1810, Spencer Perceval, the Prime Minister, the only one assassinated in modern British history, introduced a Regency Bill, based on Pitt's Bill of 1788. The Regency Act passed on 5 February 1811, with royal assent signified by a commission, and George, Prince of Wales was sworn in as Regent on 6 February. The Act and the resulting oaths emphasised the possibility of recovery and for the first year, at the insistence of Perceval, and against the wishes of the Whigs, the prince's powers were accordingly limited. George's care was entrusted to Charlotte under the Regency Act, but it was a trying responsibility, and one the queen found increasingly difficult, not least as he aged. The deterioration of his condition in July 1811 meant that he was physically restrained. Despite the opiates he was given in the form of laudanum, sleep proved difficult, while he ate little, and his awareness of the world around him was limited. This included such triumphs as the battles of Salamanca and Waterloo, and also a major gain in prestige. Royal status for the Electorate of Hanover, proclaimed by the Prince Regent in October 1814, was swiftly recognised by the Congress of Vienna, and Hanover also gained territory, becoming the fourth largest state in the German Confederation of 1815 after Austria, Prussia and Bavaria.

The king died in seclusion, if not obscurity, in his room overlooking the North Terrace at Windsor, of pneumonia, on the evening of 29 January 1820, aged eighty-two. Having lain in state for two days, he was buried in St George's Chapel on 16 February, returning to a building on which he had lavished so much attention. Large numbers attended the funeral of a man who had seen so much history and who had been the king of the overwhelming majority for their entire lives.

GEORGE IV

It was somehow appropriate that George IV, who was ill with pleurisy, was not the chief mourner at his father's funeral, a role instead taken by York. In truth, it did not matter. A Duke of York in such a place was not going to be the basis for a royal coup, in some sort of repetition of 1460, 1461, 1471 and 1483, while the antipathy between George IV and his father, while repeatedly difficult, had been less traumatic politically than the comparable rifts under George I and George II. Separately, the idea of a monarch deploying force to achieve his own goals at the assumptions and aspirations focused on Parliament would have seemed bizarre. Radical critics made hostile comparisons, but it was the king-in-Parliament, not the king alone, that was the centre of such criticism, as had also been the case for the American Patriots.

Born in 1762, the future George IV became king at fifty-seven, having waited longer than virtually any previous heir to become monarch, although not as long as William IV, Edward VII and Charles III were to do. As a result, George became king not only long after he was estranged from his wife, but also after the death of his only legitimate child, and at a time when he increasingly suffered health problems. George's alienation from his father had added to the sense of exasperation and urgency with which he pursued the trappings of monarchy. This had been very obvious during the Regency Crisis of 1788–9.

George was not a man able effectively to resist the trend toward a lesser political role for the monarch, however much he might spasmodically insist on his views of his own importance. His stamina was already weakened by his weight, poor health, laziness and self-indulgence, the last reflecting the degree to which George lacked his father's strong sense of duty, as well as his moral concern. The Prince Regent also did not have the political ability to manage scandal in any effective way.

A Change of Kings

'How much better is it to weep over departed excellence in the nearest and dearest of all connections than to be harassed by living profligacy.'

Henry Addington, Viscount Sidmouth,
Home Secretary, 1820, on Georges III and IV

Conscious of the military reputation enjoyed or adopted by other monarchs, George IV liked to set a military tone, and commanded the Prince of Wales's Regiment of Light Dragoons. His pretensions could verge on the ridiculous, especially in 1811 when he made himself Field Marshal, designing a uniform in scarlet that, with its weighty gold embroidery, was reported to weigh 200 pounds, and in which he was buried. In 1792 and 1814, he had himself painted in uniform, and later in life liked to tell people that he had been at the battle of Waterloo and would seek confirmation from Arthur, Duke of Wellington, winning the tactful reply: 'So you have told me, Sir.'

Having been closely linked politically and socially to the Whigs as a young man, George shifted his position from 1807. In part, this reflected changes in British politics, but he also became more conservative, with a greater concern about the Church of England and an opposition to the Whigs' pressure for negotiations with France. As Prince Regent from 1811, George did not want to accept the restrictions of the Regency Act, but was outmanoeuvred by Spencer Perceval, the Prime Minister, who was stronger in Parliament. Perceval's assassination led Robert, 2nd Earl of Liverpool, to become Prime Minister. Although posing difficulties in his petulance, George followed his father in stressing his patriotism, duty and wish for an inclusive ministry. In his first message to the Cabinet after he assumed his full powers in 1812, George stated his wish to pursue goals 'common to the whole nation'.

The Whigs accused George of being a turncoat and overly influenced by Tory associates, notably Isabella, Marchioness of Hertford, but this underestimated George's capacity to make his own decisions. In 1812, George tried to bring the Whigs into what he hoped would be a widely inclusive ministry, but he refused to accept their liberal views on Catholic Emancipation and the war. He also, with familiarity, became satisfied with the ministers he had inherited, a course eased by the competence of Liverpool as Prime Minister.

A supporter of the government during the war with Napoleon and of the post-war socio-political discontent, George created problems in 1820 when wishing to divorce his first cousin Caroline of Brunswick-Wolfenbüttel, whom he had married in 1795 but who had left him in 1797 due to his boorishness and infidelity. In 1820, her cause was taken up by radicals, while ministers sought to avoid public scandal. The entire episode was very different from that which had faced George I, not least because it was played out in Britain, whereas George I's difficulties with his adulterous wife Sophia Dorothea had been contained to Germany, occurred twenty years before he came to the throne, and had been largely private. She was held in house-imprisonment.

The small majority in the House of Lords for the divorce Bill led the government to withdraw it rather than face a stormy passage in the Commons, much to the fury of George, but he benefited from growing popular disquiet about Caroline's personal life, especially the evidence that she had had affairs with foreign servants. As a result, the Commons rejected by a large majority an opposition motion that Caroline's name be restored to the liturgy. She was also refused entry to the lavish coronation that George had planned. The crown was enhanced by an unprecedented high number of borrowed jewels, and George wore ornate and heavy clothes. These included on his entry into Westminster Abbey, a black velvet hat carrying a large plume of ostrich feathers from which a heron's plume emerged. His gold-bordered crimson velvet train was so long and heavy that nine pages were needed to support it. Although radical sentiment remained strong, there had also been a rallying of support to George by the time of his coronation. Caroline died three weeks later, George remarking on 'the blessing which the protecting Hand of God, in his mercy, has bestowed upon me, in this recent event . . . it has literally turned one almost quite topsy turvy'.

Feasting Loyalty

'I verily believe there exists throughout the nation a spirit of loyalty unparalleled for many years. In most places, measures were taken to make the lower orders substantially feel the importance of the day; they were feasted with what they seldom taste, and that most plentifully. Such language speaks home to them intelligibly, and the remembrance of the festival and of the occasion will be indelible.'

George Huntingford, Bishop of Hereford, 1821. Huntingford benefited in his clerical career from his friendship with Addington

---

George's coronation was followed in 1821–2 by highly popular visits to Ireland, Hanover and Scotland; the first to Ireland and Scotland by the monarch since the seventeenth century. In Wales, he only visited Thomas Burgess at Abergwili near Carmarthen and Plas Newydd, the seat of the Marquess of Anglesey, en route to Dublin, as he had continued the Hanoverian pattern of having no inauguration ceremony as Prince of Wales. George's visit to Ireland saw him at his best, able to respond to people and circumstances and to present himself in a benign and accessible fashion. Very much enjoying the fuss, George conspicuously associated himself with Irish themes: on his royal entry into Dublin, he carried a hat decorated with a big bunch of shamrock, while he requested the wearing of Irish goods at the drawing room held in the Viceregal Lodge. A triumph of showmanship, George's visit enabled him to see his mistress, Elizabeth, Lady Conyngham; he visited her twice at Slane.

Adopting a similar stance to his father, George, however, showed no willingness to respond to the address from the Catholic bishops and move toward Catholic Emancipation. Indeed, a careful distinction was drawn between the addresses from the Established Church, Dublin Corporation and the University of Dublin which were to be presented to George while he was on the throne. In contrast, those from the Presbyterians, the Catholic bishops and the Quakers were presented in the Closet, ie. privately.

The last stage of George's trip was spoiled by poor health – 'an attack in his bowels' – and by George's anger about the movement of Caroline's body through London. Sidmouth complained:

> The king is in a very uncomfortable state of mind. The circumstances attending the Queen's funeral he is frequently recurring to, in a manner which shows a degree of chagrin, and irritation beyond what I have ever observed in him. These feelings have not affected his general behaviour, and deportment, so as to attract the observation, except of a very few; the actual expression of them has not been so confined, and limited as could be wished.

Having returned from Ireland, George swiftly moved on to Hanover. In Brussels, en route, his ability as a mimic enlivened dinner with William I of the Netherlands. In Hanover, George's skill in making himself agreeable to a new audience was seen with his facility in speaking German, but his precarious health hit. He had to convalesce, but soon recovered sufficiently to take part in the social round expected of him, a round that is reminiscent of the social pressures of modern kingship:

> The King is well enough to receive company at dinner – Tomorrow he will have audiences – Friday he is to visit his stud, and manege, which is upon a very large scale, and on Saturday His Majesty will take leave by showing himself at the theatre. As the King proposes to stop at Gottingen on his way the disappointment occasioned by his illness will have been in some measure repaired.

In an echo of the past, George's visit provided an opportunity for diplomatic discussion with other leading figures, as the Austrian Chancellor Metternich visited Hanover. However, as a sign of the times, Metternich was there to see Robert, 2nd Marquess of Londonderry, the Foreign Secretary. Whereas on the last visit by a monarch, that by George II in 1755, the king had played a central role in the negotiations handled at Hanover, that was no longer the case.

In 1822, George continued by visiting Scotland. He sailed in his yacht, the *Royal George*, from Greenwich to Leith, and back from Queensferry, and therefore he did not have to face the long journey through England. As a sign of changing times, steam tugs were used to help the *Royal George* cope with contrary winds, but in Scotland George visited Newbattle Abbey, the seat of the Marquess of Lothian, and not Glasgow. Aside from wearing Highland dress of a lavish and very expensive type, George, on his visit, also favoured Scottish music and dances, as well as Glenlivet and Atholl Brose; the previous year, he had enjoyed Irish whiskey punch. What George made of the sermon he heard preached by the

Moderator of the Church of Scotland, against lust and in favour of marital harmony, is unknown, but George was accustomed to the consequences of his position as a public defender of the moral order. The expectation that George's reception in Edinburgh, as in Dublin and Hanover, would be more favourable than in London, the centre of English disaffection, was proved correct.

After his tour of his kingdoms, however, George retreated from the public face of monarchy and, after 1823, made no public appearances in London except for the ceremonial opening and proroguing of Parliament. Instead, he spent most of his time at his favourite haunts of Brighton and Windsor, much of it in the company of his mistress, Elizabeth, Lady Conyngham. The daughter of a self-made Yorkshire businessman, she was considered a parvenue and a gold-digger. She replaced Lady Hertford as favourite in late 1819 and gave George, who was initially intoxicated by her, a new optimism. Her husband's appointment as Lord Steward of the Household in 1821, the year in which her relationship with George was closest, aided their contact, although propriety was maintained to the extent of George and Elizabeth not living under the same roof. Nevertheless, the lavish presents and clear public regard that George showed for Lady Conyngham were such that the relationship was no secret. Indeed, the king insisted that she sit close to him throughout the coronation. Her presence was rewarded with repeated looks that struck some as indecent.

She, however, was peremptory and could irritate the king, who was to complain that she bored him. He was quite easily bored. George's affections were not restricted to her, although, with increasing age, he seems to have been seeking affectionate company rather than sex; indeed, Lady Conyngham was no youngster: she was fifty-seven in 1823. They continued their relationship until his death.

In July 1822, George wrote as 'a most affectionate friend' from Carlton House, possibly to a 'Mrs M.'; the recipient is unclear:

You may easily imagine, warm & sincere as my affections are towards you, I have had but little rest, since we separated last night. The [sic] feel, that I may, possibly & unfortunately in a hurried moment, when my mind & Heart being torn in fifty different ways from fifty different causes have let an unjust or a hasty expression escape me to any one (but most especially to You, who I so *truly love* & who are so *invaluable* to *Me* as my *friend*) is to *me*, a sensation much *too painful* to be *endured*; therefore, let me *implore* of You, to come to me, *be it but for a moment*, the *very first thing* you do this morning, for I shall hate myself until I have the opportunity of expressing *personally* to You, those pure & Genuine feelings of affection for You, which will never cease to live in *my Heart*, so long as that Heart, itself continues to beat. I am much too unhappy to say more . . .

One of the reasons why George showed himself so rarely in London in his later years as king was that he was very unpopular there. Yet, he also felt ridiculous as a result of his girth, and was affected by poor health, the latter two problems later seen with Edward VII. Indeed, he had been badly ill with a chest infection when he became king. Sidmouth noted: 'The situation of his present Majesty was extremely alarming during the greater part of Tuesday night: but the formidable symptoms have gradually given way, and all apprehensions of a fatal result appear to be over.' The fear, however, of 'a fresh attack, to resist which his constitution may have become unequal' led to action: 'The quantity of blood taken from him in the course of twelve or thirteen hours by the advice of Dr. Tierney was enormous, and to that advice the preservation of H.M.'s life is, through the blessing of Providence, to be ascribed.' Ten days later he added: 'The King's health gradually improves but there are very painful obstacles to a rapid recovery.' Renewed ill-health led Liverpool to note in July 1820, 'The King's progress to recovery is but slow.'

Notably due to the death of Princess Charlotte, his only child, George's life was sad. His reign moreover was, at times, a ludicrous postlude to the great days of his career, when, as the leader of fashionable society, he had created a new, alternative image of royalty and a new standard of English and international elegance: the Brighton Pavilion stands today as testimony to his idiosyncratically high sense of taste, but this was no longer the prince who had built so grandly and strove in his own fashion to compete with Napoleon. Initially, as Prince of Wales, George's building had essentially been for private purposes, and was decorative, rather than a work of state. Carlton House on Pall Mall, which George had been granted in 1783 as his first independent residence, required restoration, but George had it extensively rebuilt by the architect Henry Holland, and the building was also lavishly decorated, providing a setting for impressive, and always expensive, entertainments. This expenditure contributed directly to the prince's debts.

Carlton House was not alone. From 1783, the prince spent summers at Brighton, newly fashionable as a result of the belief that sea bathing was healthy. Needing a residence, George had a house transformed into a villa by 1787. Subsequently, the Brighton Pavilion was enhanced, with fresh construction and exuberant decoration. The Dome, built from 1804, was designed in what was seen as an Indian fashion, and the metamorphosis of what had been a classical villa into an oriental pleasure palace was also accomplished by the furnishings, which again were in an Indian style. As king, George was responsible for the rebuilding of Buckingham House and also supported Nash, the architect there, in his work on what became Regent's Park and on the building of Regent Street. George supported Wyatville in the rebuilding of Windsor Castle.

Initially as king, George showed himself in considerable style. The list of courtiers and servants requiring lodging at Phoenix Park in Dublin in 1821 was impressive:

His Majesty – requiring for his private apartments a Bedroom, a Sitting room adjoining, and a Page's waiting room.

4 Pages of the Backstairs in constant attendance
4 Pages of the presence (2nd class of servants)
4 Footmen

Sir Benjamin Bloomfield
Valet
2 Footmen

Equerry in Waiting
1 servant

Gentlemen of the Wine Cellar, Confectioner, Pastry Cook, 2 Master Cooks, Table Decker, and from 10 to 12 Cooks and servants belonging to the Kitchen.

The above must be lodged where the King resides.

The Lord Steward of His Majesty's Household
The Lord Chamberlain
The Master of the Horse
The Groom of the Stole
4 Valets and 8 Footmen

4 Lords of the Bedchamber
4 Valets and 4 Footmen

4 Grooms of the Bedchamber
8 Equerries and Aidedecamps
4 Gentlemen Ushers
16 Servants

Secretary to the Lord Steward
1 Clerk
1 Servant

Secretary to the Lord Chamberlain
1 Clerk
1 Servant

Clerk Comptroller of the Kitchen
1 Servant
3 Clerks

2nd Gentleman of the Wine Cellar
2nd Confectioner and his Assistant
2nd Table Decker
3 Silver Scullery Men
4 Principal Cooks
3 Apprentices

Physician, Surgeon, and Apothecary to the Person
20 Gentlemen Pensioners and 4 Officers

Stable Department – numbers not known.

Once he became reclusive, George cut a far less impressive figure, but he still spent heavily, including on German musicians and French cooks, and had five yachts.

Like his father, George's range of interests was impressive. He founded the Royal Society for Literature and chartered twenty-five other bodies in his reign including the Royal Asiatic Society, the Society of Geology, Edinburgh Academy, McGill University in Canada, St David's College Lampeter and King's College London. Bishop Burgess said that George ought to be remembered for these more than other things. He backed the Literary Fund's support for indigent writers, had literary interests, secured the return of the Stuart papers to Britain, sponsored the copying of a collection of papyri found at Herculaneum, and was interested in animals. His menagerie reflected the spreading sway of British power and included kangaroos, an ostrich, a zebra, a leopard and the giraffe presented in 1827 by Mehmet Ali, the Pasha of Egypt.

Politically, George benefited from the stability of the Liverpool ministry (1812–27), in much the same way that George III had benefited from that of Pitt the Younger. After Liverpool had a stroke and retired in April 1827, however, George found politics troubling. The crisis of Liverpool's succession was resolved by making George Canning head of the government, against the initial wishes of the king, but Canning's death that August reopened the political situation. Keen not to turn to Wellington, whom he distrusted politically, the even-more-than normally petulant George helped to put in a government under Frederick, Viscount Goderich, a former Chancellor of the Exchequer. However, the agreeable Goderich was weak and could not control his colleagues. Disillusioned with Goderich, whose willingness to blubber did not impress the king, George accepted his resignation in January 1828, and finally turned to Wellington. George insisted that the government should not push through Catholic Emancipation; indeed he had obliged Canning to appoint a Chief Secretary for Ireland who did not support Emancipation.

Wellington, however, saw Emancipation as necessary, and pressed George hard on the issue, urging him to ignore the contrary advice of his brother, Ernest, Duke of Cumberland. As George, who, in his anger, threatened Wellington with abdication, had no alternative ministers to turn to, he finally agreed, under pressure from the duke, to sign the Catholic Relief Act on 13 April 1829. The willingness of George to bow to necessity defined this last stage of his reign, but it left him bitter and deflated.

George might have been earlier termed the 'First Gentleman in Europe', but, as monarch, he lacked charisma and was widely believed to have no sense of integrity; although he has recently benefited from sympathetic reassessment. His reign was a lost opportunity for assertive monarchy. In some respects, the history of the British monarchy has often been such. James I and VI failed to unify England and Scotland, and his Stuart successors found it impossible to create a domestic consensus or to win glory abroad, while the 'Glorious Revolution' did not produce an uncontested succession, nor lead to the accession of vigorous monarchs with children. Whereas Georges I, II and III were not without success, under George IV, especially after the royal visit to Scotland, the British monarchy blatantly lacked flair, and George himself acquired a general and sustained unpopularity that was greater than that of the earlier Hanoverians. No later British monarchs, including Edward VIII on his abdication in 1936, had been so unpopular on the eve of his or her death as George was when he died on 26 June 1830.

The deaths of his brother Edward in 1820, and even more so, Frederick in 1827, had an effect on George, helping turn his hypochondria toward thoughts of mortality. These deaths also brought problems to sort out. Thus, Wellington wrote to George's confidant, Sir William Knighton, after Frederick's death:

> Before I would take charge of the enclosed paper I was made certain that there was no male by which the unfortunate person to whom it related could bring under His Majesty's notice unless I could interest you in her favour; and I shall not think it proper that I should know of the circumstances therein stated without at least giving you the option of laying before the King, knowing as I do His Majesty's affection for his late brother, and how keenly he feels everything that can affect his reputation and honour.

Close to his end George was very sickly and heavily drugged with laudanum, but he still ate copiously and pursued a variety of interests. Alongside concern about racing, including eagerness for news of the results of races and for details about horses he wished to buy, came signs of religious devotion. George read the Bible frequently, took solace in receiving the sacrament, and declared his repentance of his youth, saying that he hoped the mercy he had shown others would be offered him. The king's decline took several months, during which he displayed considerable courage and calm. In his last moments, he looked at Sir Watkin Waller, who was holding his hand, and said 'My boy, this is death!' He then fell back dead in his chair; the rupture of a blood vessel in his stomach had killed him.

The funeral, in Windsor on 15 July, saw few signs of grief. The Unitarian *Monthly Repository's* obituary declared: 'He was too regardless of the decorum which his father so steadily maintained for it to be decent in religionists to become his apologists.' George left his plate and jewels to Lady Conyngham but she turned down the entire legacy. Living until 1861, she was excluded from Court by both William IV and Victoria.

WILLIAM IV

William IV's reign (1830–7) can be seen as beginning the process of revival that was to culminate in the development of imperial splendour under Victoria and Edward VII. Born on 21 August 1765 in Buckingham Palace, William was the third son of George III and Queen Charlotte. His father decided that he should enter the navy, making plans to that end in 1778, and William did so in 1779, beginning as an able seaman and (in 1780) becoming a midshipman. George III was keen that naval life should not mean that William acquired inappropriate habits, and distance did not prevent him from keeping an eye on William, as on his other children. Indeed, in 1779, George arranged that Henry Majendie, whose father John had instructed Queen Charlotte in English and been tutor to the Prince of Wales and the Duke of York, should teach William on board the *Prince George*. Majendie was listed as a midshipman. In 1781, Majendie was to be appointed William's Preceptor; he clearly commended himself to George, becoming a canon of Windsor in 1785, vicar of Windsor and a canon of St Paul's in 1798, and Bishop of Chester in 1800.

However, in 1780, William caused concern by disorderly behaviour in London, leading George to have him returned to his ship.

In 1781, George III wrote of 'the anxiety I have for the success of my endeavours to fit my children for the various stations they may fill, and that they may be useful and a credit to their family'; and concern about William led George to write in 1783 to Colonel Richard Grenville, Governor for Frederick, Duke of York, then residing in Germany as Prince-Bishop of Osnabrück, which was under partial Hanoverian control:

> I hope speedily to send William to Germany not thinking this a safe place on many accounts for one of his age and not less so who by having been two years abroad must expect more liberty than I can approve on this side of the water . . . Frederick has succeeded so well that his example cannot be too closely followed . . . William is rather giddy and has rather too much the manners of his profession [the navy], polishing and composure are the ingredients wanting to make him a charming character.

The following year, George wrote to William:

> I am glad you propose being more regular in your correspondence, it is impossible you cannot want for topics if you take pains to improve your mind; the natural attendance whilst at sea certainly was no advantage to your manners nor could your education be so closely followed as could be wished either in your station as a prince or as an officer for seamanship is but a very small part of the requisites necessary in superior commands and for want of which the service has on many opportunities most fatally suffered. The knowledge of the springs that actuate men is necessary to know how to turn them to the pursuits that are honorable to themselves or of utility to the state;

that you may by diligence become what it must be your own desire as well as that of those who wish you well will ever be my objective.

Over the following decade, the young William received social and professional promotion. Created Earl of Munster and Duke of Clarence and St Andrews in 1789, William, who had only been promoted to be lieutenant in 1785, became a rear-admiral in 1790, a vice-admiral in 1794, an admiral in 1799 and, in 1811, admiral of the fleet, and thus commander-in-chief, a step that blocked the promotion of other officers. It was not until 1821, when George IV promoted John, 1st Earl of St Vincent, a distinguished veteran of the French Revolutionary War, that there was a second such commander. In 1827, William was made Lord High Admiral, a post created for him.

The late eighteenth and early nineteenth centuries were the period of British naval triumph and hegemony, for which, however, the Duke of Clarence was not responsible. He had seen active service during the War of American Independence, off Gibraltar, in the West Indies, the Channel and in North American waters, and commanded ships in peacetime in 1786–90, acquiring a reputation as a martinet. Appointed captain of the *Pegasus* in 1786, William quarrelled over discipline with his experienced first lieutenant Isaac Schomberg, leading to Schomberg applying unsuccessfully for a court-martial and then being superseded. In 1788, William transferred to the *Andromeda*, and, in 1790, to the *Valiant* which was part of the fleet assembled as war seemed likely with Spain over competing claims on what became the coast of British Columbia. However, Spain backed down, ensuring that William did not gain wartime experience. He was not to be given command during the French Revolutionary and Napoleonic Wars. William also acquired a preference for alcohol and smoking from his naval life, as well as a bluff manner with rough speech; anticipating George V and

George VI with the naval background, smoking and, in the case of George V, bluffness.

George's reign was so unedifying that the ascent of William to the throne in 1830 was seen as a relief. Despite his own failings, and there were many, his reputation was enhanced by being compared to his unlamented brother. The size and cost of the court was cut and the public allowed onto the East Terrace at Windsor Castle.

Thanks to his impulsive and well-meaning personality, William, who could also be very angry, was frequently ebullient and somewhat eccentric: his conversations went off at a tangent, leading him to be dubbed 'Silly Billy'. Having become king, William did not throw off his unbuttoned style. He regarded himself as a friend of his brother George, but displayed scant grief during his funeral, instead talking loudly and leaving before the coffin had been laid in the vault. At one level, William's lack of dignity was the result of a welcome (to some) openness and bumptious eccentricity, but there were echoes of his father's behaviour when ill. William enjoyed walking round London without show or ceremony, but had to be dissuaded from doing so and from his habit of inviting new acquaintances to dinner at the palace. His coronation was far less grand than that of George: there was no state banquet in the evening. Rather than residing in Buckingham Palace, William continued to live in Clarence House, which was more modest. A democratic myth grew up about William because his easy-going nature was confused with an inclination toward political life. William did not travel abroad as monarch, and was not therefore associated with Hanover.

William's love life was rich and varied, but he was genuinely attached to the actress Dorothy Jordan with whom he lived publicly from 1790 to 1811, having ten children, the eldest of whom was created Earl of Munster in 1831. After the death of the Prince Regent's young daughter, Charlotte, in 1817, William, at fifty-two, married a wife appropriate to his station in the

succession as George III's third son, with the elder two now childless: Adelaide, elder daughter of Duke George of Saxe-Meiningen.
To save bother and presumably expense, William and his brother,
Edward, Duke of Kent, the fourth son, were married at the same
time in a double wedding at Kew Palace in 1818. Adelaide had two
miscarriages and bore William two daughters, but both died in
infancy, one, in 1820, after only a few hours; the other, Princess
Elizabeth, in 1821, aged only three months. A good sort, denied
any outlet for her maternal instincts, Adelaide was a kind stepmother to William's children by Dorothy Jordan.

A Popular William

'He walked up St James Street the other day quite alone, the
mob following him, and one of the common women threw
her arms round him and kissed him.'

Mrs Arbuthnot, *Journal*, 21 July 1830

The contrast between the large number of pubs named after
William and the small number named after George is instructive.
William was seen as wanting to be a 'constitutional' monarch –
which, indeed, he sought to be. Unlike George, William had no
prejudice against the Whigs, and had been willing to cooperate
with Charles, 2nd Earl Grey's attempt to form a ministry in 1830.
William's concessions to the Whigs during the crisis had been
offered grudgingly, but, when faced with the prospect of incur-
ring the wrath of the populace by thwarting reform, William's
tendency was to give way. His alleged support for the Franchise
Reform Bill was used extensively, and to considerable effect, by
supporters of reform in the 1831 election, while, more generally,
William's service to the state was popular: mainly his naval
service, but also to a lesser extent his ultimate flexibility over
reform. William certainly benefited from the popularity of the

navy. William's opposition to reform in 1832 was blamed on his wife, Queen Adelaide, his brother Cumberland, or his sisters – but not on the king himself.

In July 1834, William asked William, 2nd Viscount Melbourne, the new Whig leader, to form a ministry, only, four months later, to dismiss this and to turn to the Tories under Sir Robert Peel. They formed a ministry in December 1834, but due to a lack of sufficient support in the House of Commons, even after a general election, it did not last, and Melbourne returned to power in April 1835. This was a repeat of the political crisis in 1783–4, but the general election had not gone as well as that for William Pitt the Younger in 1784.

VICTORIA

The sickly William, afflicted by asthma and arthritis, was succeeded in 1837 by Victoria, the daughter of the dead Edward, Duke of Kent. She had been in effect adopted by William and Adelaide as the daughter they could not have. William was determined to survive until Victoria, whom he liked, came of age, so that her mother, the Duchess of Kent, should not be Regent. He succeeded in his objective, dying four weeks after this coming of age. Moreover, thanks in part to this, Victoria's accession was popular. She was eighteen, short, keen on riding, blue-eyed, and a laughing young woman who knew little about monarchy. Rejecting the influence of her unloved mother, Victoria became close to the Prime Minister, the gossipy William, 2nd Viscount Melbourne, who explained much about the nature of British politics and about what she would have to do as Queen. Melbourne also added the role of royal private secretary to that of Prime Minister, which created the possibility of a conflict of interests, and Victoria responded very emotionally when Melbourne briefly resigned on losing his parliamentary backing in 1839. There was already tension over the queen's hostility to Lady Flora Hastings, an unmarried lady-in-waiting to her mother who, as the result of an abdominal growth, Victoria thought pregnant, which was not the case.

The treatment of Hastings led to a public scandal, which broadened out into a political crisis when Victoria refused to dismiss the Whig ladies of her bedchamber as requested by Robert Peel who was trying to organise a Tory government. Victoria followed Melbourne's advice to refuse Peel's request, and Peel, unable to form a government, left the way open to Melbourne's return. This was constitutionally serious as Victoria had acted in a highly partisan fashion, preventing the creation of a ministry she did not want. Separately, Hastings died, probably of cancer. Victoria ended the crises of 1839 unpopular, and eating too much in order to cope with the stress.

Victoria brought to the fore many of the tendencies of diligent rulership and piety seen with George III, but was also part of a more general trend, certainly clear in comparison with Continental monarchies, toward a careful stance in politics, and notably that of accommodation. Although all very different, the combination of the elderly and ailing George III, the sensual George IV, the caution of William IV about reaction, the methodical constitutionalism of Victoria, and sensualism redux in the case of Edward VII, was such that the continued role of monarchy in politics and government became far less proactive.

Victoria was to take the prestige of monarchy to its highest point when, in 1876, the title of Empress of India was created for her by the Royal Titles Act. Prince Albert had suggested to Victoria in 1843 that she gain the title of Empress of India, but it was Benjamin Disraeli who brought Victoria's wish to fruition. This creation was a counterpoint to Wilhelm I becoming Emperor of Germany in 1871, which would have left Victoria's daughter, the wife of Wilhelm's heir, Victoria's superior in precedence, and an establishment of a new peak and focus for imperial prestige. At the same time, the title was an instance of the observation in *Good*

Words in 1886 by Dinah Mulak Craik that 'working women in all ranks, from our Queen downwards, are, and ought to be, objects of respect to the entire community'. Imperial position was a counter to the criticism surrounding Victoria's withdrawal from public life after the death of Prince Albert.

It is more apt to wind back to *Windsor Castle in Modern Times* (1841–3), a painting by Edwin Landseer (1802–73), Victoria's favourite painter. A contrast with the medievalism, although not with the hunting round Windsor beloved by George III, this showed Victoria and Albert as an idealised family with the gardens of Windsor Castle visible through the open window. Albert has just been shooting, but the dead birds on the carpet do not bleed, and have no visible signs of injury. Everybody is appropriate and devoted, including the dogs. Franz Xavier Winterhalter's *The Royal Family in 1846* offered the same impression.

Victoria and Albert

'She is certainly an odd woman; her devotion and submission to her husband seem to know no bounds. When first she married Melbourne told her she must not expect her domestic happiness never to be ruffled. She did not like this at all. But it never has. Albert never looks at her handsome ladies and maids of honour. He is absorbed with other objects, is full of ambition and the desire of governing and having political influence. He has attained this object for he and the Queen are now *one* with the ministers, with these as well as with the last.'

Charles Greville, *Memoirs*, 26 January 1848

Victoria's marriage, the fuss over which did not impress Charles Dickens, who had no emotional commitment to monarchy and who gleefully cited xenophobic popular hostility to the match, was much happier than those of the élite depicted by Dickens. The lucky princeling, Albert of Saxe-Coburg-Gotha (1819–61), his case pushed hard by his uncle, the influential Leopold, King of the Belgians, was a happy case of dynastic choice becoming love-match, and the couple were married in 1840. He was an ardent husband whose life with Victoria was surprisingly passionate for those who think that Victorian values means sexual repression. The couple had nine children, seven in the first ten years of marriage. She, however, did not enjoy being pregnant and was not kind to her eldest boy, the future Edward VII.

Rapidly educating himself in the details of the political system, Albert sought influence, but emphasised the need for the Crown to adopt political neutrality, and helped lessen Victoria's highly partisan preference for the Melbourne Whig ministry, which was necessary as Tory popularity revived. He was against public partisanship by the Crown, which had become dangerous after the political defeats of 1829–41, notably Sir Robert Peel's Conservative victory in the 1841 election. However, Albert was not against covert politics by the Palace. In fact, he encouraged it, in support of Peel as Prime Minister and, then, over the Corn Laws, against the Conservatives from 1846, and against Henry, 3rd Viscount Palmerston, as Foreign Secretary (1846–51) as too anti-German. Indeed, Victoria and Albert helped Lord John Russell to sack Palmerston in 1851, the year in which she opened the Great Exhibition.

The following year, Victoria and Albert supported the creation of a coalition government under George, 4th Earl of Aberdeen, a Peelite. Some politicians saw Albert's covert interference as unconstitutional and his hostility to Palmerston led to much press criticism. In the event, in 1859, Palmerston, rather than Russell, was selected by Victoria as Prime Minister after her failure to have Lord Granville chosen. Crucially, Albert did his dynastic duty by fathering many children, and thus avoiding the danger of the unpopular Ernest, Duke of

Cumberland, George III's fifth son and Victoria's uncle, being next in line for the throne: Ernest inherited that of Hanover in 1837 as there was no female succession there, dying in 1851 to be succeeded by his son George V, the last king of Hanover, which was annexed by Prussia in 1866 without Britain interfering.

Albert was also active in a host of spheres across public life. His prestige, drive and tact helped make him a sound committee man, and, through his position as the chairman of committees, he helped drive forward the cause of national improvement. Thus, after Parliament burned down, Albert was appointed as Chairman of the Royal Commission that was formed to choose frescoes to decorate the inside of the new Parliament buildings. He supported using the rebuilding as an opportunity to promote British arts.

More dramatically, Albert played a major role, not least as President of the Society for Arts from 1843, in promoting the Great Exhibition. In 1846, he told a deputation that 'to wed mechanical skill with high art is a task worthy of the Society of Arts and directly in the path of its duty'. In contrast, George IV had sponsored high art, most flamboyantly with the highly deco-rated Royal Pavilion in Brighton, but not mechanical skill. Albert's visit to Birmingham in 1843 developed the affirmation of a link between monarchy, industry and modernity. Due to radical agita-tion, Albert was advised not to visit the city, but he did so, touring five major factories and being favourably received.

Although he struck Dickens as 'a good example of the best sort of perfectly commonplace man, with a considerable desire to make money', Albert was a self-conscious moderniser, willing to work hard in order to acquire the detailed knowledge necessary to understand how best to implement change successfully. He was a practical paternalist, keenly committed to improvement, and concerned to lessen social discontents. At a meeting of the Society for Improving the Condition of the Working Classes in 1848, Albert argued that progress would not come from revolution and that the wealthy had a duty to help. He was committed to the improvement of public health and policing.

Victoria certainly valued order, not least in the precepts and practice of religion that mattered so much to her. Although a devout Anglican, Victoria was ready to attend Presbyterian services in Scotland, where she was head of that established church, and Lutheran services in Germany, and she saw herself equally as the monarch of all her subjects, whether Hindu, Jewish or of any other faith. Her Proclamation to the People of India of 1858 repudiated any right or desire to impose on the faith of her subjects and promised all, irrespective of religion, the rights of law.

However, Victoria had a consistent theme in preferring clerics who shied away from enthusiasm of any type, including the Anglo-Catholicism of the Oxford Movement. She varied in her response to Catholicism. Pedro V of Portugal (1853–61) pleased her when he visited Osborne House, because, although he went to Mass, he criticised the ignorance and immorality of Portuguese society and praised Britain. In her early years, she had been conciliatory and, in 1850, Victoria declared that she could not bear to hear violent abuse of Catholics. She told her children not to share in the 'vulgar prejudice' against Catholics. In 1848 the British government had offered Pius IX asylum on Malta when he was faced by serious disturbances in Rome. In 1868, Victoria visited a Catholic mass in Switzerland. Victoria's position then hardened and by the early 1870s her private attitude was some-what like that of a Protestant crusader; she strongly disapproved of conversions to Catholicism, for example those of the 3rd Marquis of Bute in 1868 and of the Marquess of Ripon in 1874. Her dislike of ritualism in the Church of England was linked to the Public Worship Act of 1874. In her final years, there was a second dramatic transformation and Victoria became in some respects a philo-Catholic. In 1887 Pope Leo XIII was allowed to send an envoy to congratulate Victoria on her Golden Jubilee: the queen was conspicuously gracious to him. On her state visits to Ireland in 1861 and 1900, Victoria met the heads of the Catholic hierarchy.

An Image of Monarchy

Modern monarchy was contextualised by references to a glorious past, references that could be highly misleading. Thus, the bronze statue of Richard I by the Italian sculptor Carlo Marochetti was placed outside the House of Lords in 1860 and captures the Lionheart well as noble warrior king. In practice, Richard spent very little time as king in England and spoke practically no English.

There were many apparent contradictions. The dynastic link with Hanover was broken in 1837, and Prince Albert's early death in 1861 cut short his influence. Albert had been a friend of the Prussian royal family and took a closer interest in European power politics than Victoria, but she still took a very close interest, turning for advice to her uncle, King Leopold I of Belgium and feeling close to his wife, Louise. They often met in the late 1830s and 1840s. Marital alliances were a key element of Victoria's diplomacy. She married her relatives into the Continental royal families and became the matriarch of the European monarchies: Kaiser Wilhelm II of Germany was her grandson. Nevertheless, despite popular jibes about the 'German' royal family, they were thoroughly English by 1900 – the claim that Edward VII, George V and Queen Mary spoke with German accents has been disproved.

George III had never gone abroad, but Victoria visited Louis-Philippe, king of France, in 1843, and, in 1845, accompanied Albert revisiting the scenes of his youth at Coburg, Gotha and Bonn, and meeting the rulers of Belgium and France. In her later years, Victoria travelled to the Continent, particularly France, almost every year; she even held a 'summit meeting' with the leading German minister, Otto von Bismarck, in 1888. Her son, Edward VII, was a frequent traveller, particularly happy in France. Like his mother, he was especially keen on Biarritz.

Travel itself became far easier for Victoria due to steam-power, the railway and the steamship carrying her across the British Isles and on many journeys in Continental Europe. As a result, Victoria was able to make British monarchy a major presence in Highland Scotland, with frequent journeys to Balmoral Castle, and Victoria enjoyed Highland games and rural quiet. She was also able to travel to northern England as her predecessors had not done, in particular visiting Sheffield in 1897, opening the new Town Hall.

At the same time, there was an imperial confidence seen in the enthusiasm surrounding Victoria's Golden and Diamond Jubilees in 1887 and 1897 respectively. In Britain and across the empire, streets, towns, geographical features and whole tracts of land were named or renamed in her honour, including the Australian state of Victoria, the city of Victoria on Vancouver Island in Canada, Victoria Falls on the Zambezi, and Lake Victoria in East Africa.

Imperial status was also part of the re-creation of Victoria in the late 1870s. She was coaxed from reclusive widowhood to a new public role by Benjamin Disraeli, who, as Prime Minister, combined imperial policies with social reform and who sought, in doing so, to foster a sense of national unity and continuity. He realised that monarchy was a potent way to lead the public and control the consequences of the spread of the franchise, a view gently mocked in Gilbert and Sullivan's comic operetta, the *Pirates of Penzance* (1879), in which the pirates, victorious over the mala-droit police, rapidly surrender at the close when summoned to do so in the name of the queen. At once an opportunistic and skilful political tactician, who was also an acute and imaginative thinker, Disraeli was able to create a political culture around the themes of national identity, national pride and social cohesion, and to focus popular support for the Conservatives on these themes as an alternative to the Liberal moral certainty in which the Liberal leader, William Ewart Gladstone, flourished. Disraeli carefully manipulated Victoria into accepting his view and playing the role he had allocated her. She allowed her favour for him, rather than Gladstone to be known, which was not prudent on her part. Indeed, Victoria was consistently and rudely hostile to Gladstone. But, more importantly, her withdrawal from public life after Albert's death was relaxed and then reversed.

More mundanely, the celebration of the queen, in jubilees and at other times, reflected existing norms. For the celebration of the Golden Jubilee in 1887 the women and children of the town of Ashby-de-la-Zouch sat down to a tea of sandwiches, bread and butter, and cake in the marketplace; while the men had earlier had a meal of roast beef, mutton, potatoes, plum pudding and beer, which had been prepared by women as meals in general were.

A Changing Political World

This was captured in Anthony Trollope's novel, *The Duke's Children* (1879–80), in which the constituents of the fictional Silverbridge were now less under the control of the Duke of Omnium, a Whig. Omnium's heir, Lord Silverbridge, is very different, a Conservative: 'We got to protect our position as well as we can against the Radicals and Communists.'

A sense of change in monarchy was scarcely surprising given the major developments in politics and government during Victoria's long reign. Hereditary monarchy remained important, though it had lost much of its power. Victoria could influence but not control politics. In his important *The English Constitution*

(1867), Walter Bagehot claimed that 'a republic has insinuated itself beneath the folds of a monarchy' and argued that the monarchy was useful as an image rather than a source of authority: 'It acts as a disguise. It enables our real rulers to change without heedless people knowing it.' He stated that the monarch had three rights, none of them commanding: 'the right to be consulted, the right to encourage, the right to warn'. More bluntly, Bagehot described Victoria as a retired widow, and her heir as an unemployed youth.

Victoria did not accept the limited part Bagehot left the monarchy, but the honorific role was to the fore, as in 1850, when Victoria opened the Royal Border Bridge over the River Tweed at Berwick. A viaduct of twenty-eight arches costing £253,000, designed by Robert Stephenson, one of the greatest engineers of the day, and still impressive today, the height of the bridge and the curve of the approach provide a fine vista. Moreover, this was a man-made vista, as those of Victoria's reign increasingly were. Proving that technology can unify the state, the bridge provided the last railway link between London and Edinburgh. Victoria also travelled on Thomas Bouch's Tay Bridge, awarding him a knighthood shortly before its deadly collapse in 1879.

Yet, the honorific role could be inappropriate. Her first cousin, George, 2nd Duke of Cambridge, was a very traditionally minded commander-in-chief of the army from 1856 to 1895. This position was in theory brought under the close control of the War Office by the War Office Act of 1870, part of the reform policy of Edward Cardwell, Secretary of State for War from 1869 to 1874. However, Cambridge's determination, connections and experience helped ensure that the Act did not have the impact that might have been anticipated. Although not directly responsible for the serious problems in the army revealed by the Boer War of 1899–1902, Cambridge had not been a reformer like Frederick, Duke of York, commander-in-chief in 1795–1809 and 1811–27.

Cambridge lost his position under a Liberal government, but the Conservatives who returned to power under Robert, 3rd Marquess of Salisbury in 1895 ensured that Victoria, who viewed them with favour, ended her reign reasonably confident in politics. Indeed, the Conservatives were re-elected in 1900.

When Victoria died, monarchy was to the fore. It had collapsed in the New World, with Brazil, Haiti and Mexico no longer empires, but, elsewhere, there were both emperors and monarchs aplenty. Of this number, there was no doubt that Britain had the most distinguished royal family, both because it was the world's leading empire and also due to the uniquely far-reaching nature of the latter. Moreover, the British constitution looked back to a long history presented in a pattern of development and with Britain seen as the continuation, by a form of imperial transfer, of the civilisational significance of Classical Rome. Victoria had contributed to this placement in part by not getting in the way.

As a consequence, it was possible for British monarchy to be seen in many ways without there being any linkage to the limitations or qualities of the individual monarch. This was to be an achievement that has not always been easy to replicate, and not least due to the celebrity aspect to culture summed up by Andy Warhol's comment on the brevity of fame.

7

The Troubles of the Modern Age

....

The twentieth century followed the very long reign of Victoria (1837–1901) with a quick series of reigns from 1901 to 1952: Edward VII, 1901–10; George V, 1910–35; Edward VIII, 1936; George VI, 1936–52. There had not been four monarchs so rapidly since 1685–1727 when there had also been four: James VII and II, William III and Mary, Anne, and George I. There was then the start of the very long reign of Elizabeth II (1952–2022). Each of the monarchs was important and yet it is possible to discuss the history of twentieth-century Britain while devoting relatively little attention to the monarchy; and most historians have done so. Indeed, in comparative terms, that would be reasonable because the monarchs were certainly less significant than their predecessors in the nineteenth century let alone the eighteenth and earlier centuries.

This then creates questions of balance and emphasis, not only within the book as a whole but also in the discussion of individual monarchs. In each case, it is possible to emphasise particular achievements or characteristics. Edward VII played a major role in improving relations with France; while, in two very difficult world wars, George V and George VI were important to national resolve. Each also helped Britain adapt to political change, in the shape of the rise of Labour to power, first in minority governments and then to a majority one. George V also played an important part in the establishment of the National Government of 1931. However, his successor, Edward VIII, proved a failure as a monarch, in large part due to the controversy surrounding his plans to marry a divorcee. Elizabeth II, in contrast, proved highly successful in maintaining an impression and reality of probity.

These individual careers have combined with a major shift in Britain's position, one that has affected the nature of monarchy. Independence for India in 1947 has led to the end of imperial monarchy, as, more generally, did the retreat from empire that began with independence for most of Ireland in 1922. Such a process could still leave the monarch with honorific roles, but they affected the situation back in Britain.

In his 1867 distinction between the efficient and the dignified parts of the constitution, Bagehot had underrated the continued power of monarchy and the House of Lords in the late nineteenth century. Nevertheless, Bagehot's distinction was valid and became more so during the twentieth century. It served as a model, and George V as Duke of York was set it to read as a way to teach him the constitution. There was no equivalent work exalting a greater role for the monarchy.

Edward VII

Born in 1841, the eldest son of Queen Victoria and Prince Albert, Prince Albert Edward, lived sixty years before succeeding to the throne in 1901 as Edward VII, nearly dying of typhoid in 1871 and surviving appendicitis shortly before his coronation. Although he took his seat in the House of Lords in 1861 after his father's death, he took little part in affairs of state, preferring the life of fashionable society, where he was a charming and popular figure, with several mistresses. Yet, Edward's involvement in the Tranby Croft baccarat case of 1891, a public controversy about cheating, brought scandal to the monarchy while highlighting Edward's raffish friends and love of the turf. He was called as a witness in the subsequent case, the first time the heir to the throne had been obliged to appear in court since

1411. Yet Edward also attended Faraday's lectures at the Royal Institution as a boy and presided at lectures there in 1891 and 1899.

As king, he promoted international relations, with Continental tours, and was fluent, like his mother, in French and German, and especially keen on France. He enjoyed visiting Biarritz, to which ministers could expect to be summoned. Edward's reign seemed redolent of greatness and girth; not for nothing was he known as Tum Tum. In 1902, Arthur Benson's words for 'Land of Hope and Glory', the first of Edward Elgar's *Pomp and Circumstance* marches, were first heard as part of the Coronation Ode. In 1863, Edward married a Danish princess, Alexandra, with whom he had six children, to whom Edward was an affectionate father. The second son, George, succeeded him as George V. Two sons had predeceased their parents, the eldest, Albert, proving distinctly rakish. An industrious adulterer, Edward made no real attempt to conceal his affairs, not even from his wife. He was as extravagant with his purse as with his prick.

Edward certainly was willing to act in what Bagehot would have seen as an unconstitutional manner, and notably so with reference to his response to advice and his willingness to initiate policy. Indeed, having waited for a long time, Edward came to the throne with some vigour. Separately, he also rejected aspects of his mother's legacy, not least by deciding to take his title from his second Christian name and not be King Albert, the choice that Victoria would have preferred. Edward also told the Prime Minister, Robert, 3rd Marquess of Salisbury, that he wanted to be consulted on all Crown appointments, as well as on Cabinet meetings, of which he expected full reports. Edward also wanted reports on parliamentary business.

At the same time, there was an establishment of ideas and practices that provided a new context. In 1905, the position of Prime Minister was formally entrenched in the constitution, while, in 1901, Arthur Balfour, then Leader of the House of

Commons, later Prime Minister in 1902–5, underlined to Edward a new role:

> The King is no longer merely King of Great Britain and Ireland . . . he is now the great constitutional bond uniting together in a single Empire communities of freemen separated by half the circumference of the globe. All the patriotic sentiment which makes such an Empire possible centres in him, or centres chiefly in him: and everything which emphasises his personality to our kinsmen across the sea must be a gain both to the Monarchy and to the Empire.

Edward interpreted this role in a bold fashion, seeking to conduct policy, and notably foreign policy, and also being willing to challenge politicians, not least in defence of his view of the constitution. However, his declining health, including bronchitis, lessened his energy and notably so from 1909, while the direction of politics pushed him onto the defensive, and particularly from 1908 when Herbert Asquith became Prime Minister, replacing Sir Henry Campbell-Bannerman, Liberal Prime Minister from 1905, whom Edward had liked. In 1898, he had been one of the pallbearers at Gladstone's funeral, much to Victoria's anger.

Edward faced a constitutional crisis in 1910 when the Conservative-dominated House of Lords resisted the Liberal government which depended on the support of Irish Nationalists and Labour. The government insisted that the Lords' veto be reduced in order to pave the way for Irish Home Rule. The Lords themselves were unlikely to pass such a Parliament Bill unless the king threatened to create a large number of Liberal peers, the same threat that had been employed in 1832 in order to push through the First Reform Act. Edward refused to make such a threat unless another election produced a clear mandate, and there was a constitutional impasse at the time of his death on 6

May after several heart attacks: his final words expressed pleasure at the success of one of his racehorses.

GEORGE V

George V (1910–36), the second son of Edward VII, was born in 1865 in Marlborough House in London, provided with a host of family names being George Frederick Ernest Albert, and began his career in the navy in 1877, seeing much of the world and notably the Empire. As he was not expected to succeed to the throne, his education was negligible. His long years in the navy, which, from 1889, included independent commands, helped make George self-reliant and a very heavy smoker, but also a marked supporter of clear boundaries and the dutiful observance of instructions. Criticism of role was not part of his tradition.

When his older brother, Albert, Duke of Clarence, 'Eddie', a slow developer and implausible Jack the Ripper, died of typhoid in 1892, George left the navy and in 1893, as Duke of York, married Mary of Teck, a German princess, daughter of Victoria's first cousin, with whom he had five sons and a daughter. Spending much of his time at York Cottage on the Sandringham estate of his father, George greatly enjoyed shooting and spent much time accordingly as a 'sporting' country gentleman. The cottage was not in a style that would have pleased Marie Antoinette, instead being a version of the numerous suburban villas of the time. George preferred this to the idea of a country mansion. In this, as in many respects, George was different to his father's favour for extravagance and fast living, although both men enjoyed blasting pheasants from the sky. Similarly, George shot many tigers when visiting India as Emperor in 1911. Somewhat differently, he was at a grand Athenaeum dinner in 1904 to honour the nation's foremost scientists.

In 1910, Liberal Prime Minister Herbert Asquith was able to persuade George V to pledge to create sufficient peers to push through the Parliament Act. This led to an election in December 1910 that produced the same configuration of MPs. The threat of a mass creation of peers then led the Conservative leaders to accept the legislation. In 1913, moreover, George ignored the advice of Edward's key adviser, Lord Esher, to dismiss the Liberal government. Instead, George proved more ductile to his ministers than Edward had been. Temperamentally a conservative, George was primarily a constitutional monarch.

In 1914, George summoned 'My loyal subjects' to take part in World War I, and during the conflict, he very much followed George III's example of decency and patriotism in the shape of active, diligent and public support for the war effort. In 1917, George changed the family name from Saxe-Coburg to Windsor.

George V saw empires disappear in China, Russia, Austro-Hungary, Germany and Turkey, and was clearly threatened by the ambitions of radical left-wing political movements. The first major blow occurred, however, in Ireland. Under the Anglo-Irish Treaty of December 1921, most of Ireland became the Irish Free State, a self-governing dominion within the British Empire, with a Governor-General appointed by the Crown. This, however, was a stopgap. In 1932, Eamon de Valera, who had been leader of Sinn Féin, gained power and successfully pressed the British to recall the Governor-General. He was replaced by a nonentity nominated by de Valera who undertook no public duties. Under a new constitution, what was now called Ireland gained a non-executive president in 1937, and, in turn, became a republic in 1949.

Perceptive about politics, or at least politicians, and full of common-sense, George had to face the issues of three-party politics, as well as the continued royal need to support particular politicians to be Prime Minister. Thus, in 1923, on the death of Andrew Bonar Law, the Conservative Prime Minister, who had not recommended a successor, George backed Stanley Baldwin rather than George, Viscount Curzon, the king arguing that a peer could not be Prime Minister in a situation changed by the Parliament Act of 1911 and the rise of Labour. George adapted to minority Labour governments in 1924 and 1929–31.

The political crisis of 1931, with the Labour Cabinet divided over the fiscal programme recommended by Ramsay MacDonald, the Prime Minister, saw George take a key role. He had already convened conferences of party leaders over Irish Home Rule in 1914 (the Buckingham Palace Conference) and again in December 1916 on the fall of Herbert Asquith as Prime Minister. In each case, as in 1931, he was a facilitator rather than active leader. He convened a conference of the party leaders which led to a National Government under MacDonald who George had pressed to stay on, a government comprising a few Labour supporters, the Conservatives and many of the Liberals. Designed to tackle the crisis, this government won solid electoral triumphs, and lasted until World War II. George was overjoyed by the National Government's election victory in 1931 and rejoiced by having a family trip to the successful musical play *Cavalcade* by Noel Coward, characteristically easy entertainment. Having told MacDonald that it was his duty to carry on, George liked the political leadership offered by MacDonald, who he favoured, and Baldwin, while he did not want Lloyd George back in power, a view in part inherited from his father.

Like his father, not someone who enjoyed books, but, unlike his father, poor at languages, George had the very quiet hobby of philately, becoming a major collector and using his royal position to acquire new issues. George was also fond of field sports, pets, the countryside, flags and uniforms, as well as shooting. He was far less keen on London, modern art and modish female fashions. He was a popular king who went on the 'Royal Tour of the North' in 1912 to visit mining communities, enjoyed speaking on the 'wireless' (radio) from 1924, and in 1932 started the annual

Christmas Day radio broadcasts. George also presented the trophy at the Wembley Cup Final from 1914. His jubilee was celebrated enthusiastically in 1935. The country could relax with George as king. Successfully married, George worried about his children, and notably his heir, but himself set a model of popular domesticity.

George V in 1935

'The King was gruff amiability itself but the visit began badly, as the royal car was too big to fit under the archway at Firle and the monarchs had to get out to walk!'

Diary of 'Chips' Channon, 1935

Unexpectedly, 1936 was to be a year of three kings. Aged seventy, George died, with radically different dying words attributed to him: 'How is the Empire?' or 'Bugger Bognor', the latter a response to the cheery suggestion that he could convalesce there. He died very popular, with nearly a million people filing past his coffin.

EDWARD VIII

George V's successor, Edward VIII, known in the royal family as David, had views of his own, over both domestic politics and foreign affairs. At home, he appeared to favour doing more to develop social cohesion. After the General Strike of 1926, Edward made a donation to the relief fund for the miners, because 'it would be an unsatisfactory end to any dispute that one side should have to give in on account of the sufferings of their dependants'. Abroad, Edward did enough to convince critics that he was sympathetic to Hitler, a sense that was to become more apparent subsequently. His father was more hostile.

Strained Relations

'He has not a single friend who is a gentleman. He does not see any decent society . . . I hardly ever see him, and don't know what he is doing.'

George V on Edward, Prince of Wales

Austen Chamberlain confided his fears of the new King-Emperor: 'he has been going downhill of late, and must pull himself together if he is to carry on the great tradition to which he is heir.' Edward's first public engagement as king was a visit to the British Industries Fair on 10 February 1936. On 4 March, he travelled to Scotland to inspect the new liner *Queen Mary* at Clydebank (a vessel he was to visit again), and he paid a surprise visit to Glasgow's slums, promising new homes. His last public appearance before the abdication crisis was his three days' tour of the depressed areas of South Wales, which began on 18 November. Part of his duties related to the military, as with the inspection of the 1st battalion of the Coldstream Guards in Windsor on 25 April, the presentation of new colours to six battalions of the Brigade of Guards on 16 July, and his inspection of RAF airfields that June.

Yet, with the somewhat vacant Edward, much was private pleasure, not only weekends with aristocrats, notably the Duke of Marlborough and the Earl of Dudley, but also a five-week Mediterranean cruise. Soon after he spent nearly a week at Balmoral and then a few days shooting at Sandringham.

Edward fell because of his determination to marry an American (twice) divorcee, Wallis Simpson, who had accompanied him on the cruise. This determination clashed with widely held expectations about the public conduct of monarchs: Britain was still a Christian society. Initially reported abroad, the news could not be kept out of the British public sphere. On 1 December

---

Princely Thoughtlessness

'Edward VIII when Prince of Wales being lunched by the Harlech golf-club, which scoured the principality for viands and vintages – and he asked for rice-pudding and lime-juice, neither of which they had. But that was either bad manners, or bad organisation by his major-domo. However we were still eating the lunch meant for him weeks afterwards.'

Lyttelton-Hart-Davis correspondence, 1960

1938, Dr A. W. F. Blunt, Bishop of Bradford, at the Bradford Diocesan Conference, made reference to the king's obligations in connection with the Coronation Service, following up a day later by remarking 'that to all outward appearance the King seems to live entirely indifferently to the public practice of religion'. The Conservative Prime Minister, Stanley Baldwin, in alliance with Archbishop Laing of Canterbury, told Edward that he had to choose, even though the Royal Marriages Act did not apply to the monarch and there was no legal basis for the Cabinet having the right to adjudication on the royal marriage. Edward, however, agreed to choose and abdicated, his radio explanation a national event. Edward's announcement of his abdication included 'The burden which constantly rests upon the shoulders of a Sovereign is so heavy that it can only be borne in circumstances different from those in which I now find myself.'

Baldwin's position was backed by the Cabinet, the Labour leadership, and the Dominion Prime Ministers. In part, there was governmental concern about Edward's views on Hitler and on unemployment, but the central issue was the proposed marriage. Democratic royalism was not compatible with government hostility. Edward reigned for ten months and twenty-one days, the shortest reign since the Norman Conquest other than that of Edward V in 1483, which was not a happy comparison.

Edward became Duke of Windsor. He was got out of France in 1940 in order to ensure that he did not pass into German hands, and parked for the remainder of the war as Governor of the Bahamas, in order to keep him under surveillance and away from undesirable elements. The duke disliked the job and displayed his characteristic racism, but he helped to tackle poverty and labour unrest.

> 'There is an immense rallying point and resilience in the British character . . . The constitution was never for one moment challenged – let that be placed to King Edward's lasting credit – and the integrity of the Crown remains unimpaired.'
>
> *Daily Telegraph*, 11 December 1936

George VI

Edward was succeeded by Prince Albert, the second son of George V. Born in 1895 at Sandringham, he went to Dartmouth Naval College and served in the navy, being present at the battle of Jutland in 1916. After leaving the navy in 1917, George spent a year in the Royal Air Force. Made Duke of York in 1920, he married Lady Elizabeth Bowes-Lyon in 1923 and they had two daughters. In his more forceful brother's shadow, he unexpectedly became king in 1936.

During World War II he helped maintain morale by staying in London during the Blitz (German air assault), rather than moving himself, or at least his family, away from risk, either elsewhere in Britain or to Canada as a large number of the wealthy did. As an instance of the ability to link up with new developments, George VI was also colonel-in-chief of the Home Guard.

Opening of Parliament, 1937

'The King seemed quite at ease, and so did the Queen . . . Once or twice he paused for a second, but on the whole he acquitted himself well, and certainly with dignity. I am told the words were especially chosen, so that he would not stammer (it is known what words give him the most difficulty. In private conversation, he always speaks easily) . . . The atmosphere was always hallowed.'

Diary of 'Chips' Channon, 12 May 1937

The Reign of George VI: A Fantasy

An anonymous work of 1763, *The Reign of George VI* presented the early twentieth century in terms of George, an ideal monarch, who comes to the throne at a time of major difficulties, not least an attempted Russian invasion. However, a number of major victories bring peace, prosperity and growth. By the 1920s, George is ruler of France and Mexico, as well as Britain and America.

Monarch and Minister

'Ernie got on particularly well with George VI for whom he had a warm regard. He was most punctilious about keeping the King informed about what was going on in the field of foreign affairs. On various occasions when I saw them together, Ernie would put a large hand on the King's back and lead him to a corner where he would tell him some story which usually evoked roars of laughter.'

Roddy Barclay, Private Secretary (1949–51)
to Ernest Bevin, Labour Foreign Secretary, 1945–51

A natural conservative, George was concerned at the plans of the Labour government elected in 1945 and also helped block the initial Labour choice of Hugh Dalton as Foreign Secretary, favouring Ernest Bevin instead. He also greatly regretted the ending of the Indian Empire. However, George was not a political player. Furthermore, he lacked the experience his father had acquired. The peacetime coalition National Government of 1931 which owed a lot to George V was not to be restored in 1945; but that was due to political circumstances rather than any failure by George VI. The new Labour government gave independence to India and Pakistan in 1947, ensuring the end of the Crown's imperial title after less than a century. Instead, George, in 1949, was given the title Head of the Commonwealth, which India had joined. A heavy smoker, in part due to social convention but also as a result of his father's example and his own spell in the navy, he faced poor health from the late 1940s and had an operation for cancer in 1951. George's last public appearance was on 31 January 1952 to see off his eldest daughter, Elizabeth, and her husband, Philip, on their tour to Australia. The king died of a coronary thrombosis six days later, aged fifty-six.

Elizabeth II

Due to her father's early death, George's elder daughter, Elizabeth II, born in 1926, (1952–2022) came to the throne early. Her own healthy lifestyle ensured a long life, one longer than that of her younger sister, Margaret, who, in contrast, was a heavy drinker and smoker and died in 2002. In 1947, Elizabeth had married her third cousin, Philip Mountbatten, who became the Duke of Edinburgh. A descendant of Victoria, he was a member of the Greek and Danish royal families. By the time of her accession, she already had children and the succession was assured. The first monarch since William IV never to have been imperial, she became Queen of the United Kingdom and of many Commonwealth countries. There was much talk of a 'New

Elizabethan Age' and a widespread optimism helped by Britain coming out of recession and the ending of rationing. Her coronation in 1953 was the cause of many households purchasing television sets or watching for the first time.

'Throughout this memorable day I have been uplifted and sustained by the knowledge that your thoughts and prayers were with me. I have been aware all the time that my peoples, spread far and wide throughout every Continent and ocean in the world, were united to support me in the task to which I have now been dedicated with such solemnity.'

The Queen's Broadcast to the
Commonwealth after her coronation

After the coronation, Elizabeth, who had been on an imperial tour when her father died in 1952, embarked on a lengthy world tour that captured the wide-ranging nature of the British world and enormous interest in the monarch. Vast crowds, for example, turned out to greet the Queen in Australian cities.

Cinema newsreels and television provided publicity for such episodes. The royal family indeed adapted to television. The Queen's first televised Christmas broadcast followed in 1957, and the wedding of Princess Margaret in 1960 was also televised.

At this stage, the Queen was very much head of what appeared to be a settled and stable society, one with relatively few challenges to her position or image. Her duties included opening Parliament and holding meetings of the Privy Council, awarding honours and decorations, and receiving visiting heads of state. Her private interests included a strong commitment to horseracing, and she was also very fond of dogs.

There was much in common between the Queen and George

III, notably a fundamental piety and, as a related factor, a strong sense of duty. Both liked country pursuits. Less happily, each had serious problems with their children and also oversaw the loss of an empire.

The 1960s brought challenges, not least the rapid loss of colonies, serious economic and fiscal problems, the development of Scottish and Welsh separatism, the outbreak of large-scale violence in Northern Ireland, and the decline of deference and turn to the 'new' linked to the Sixties, a change not restricted to that decade. There was also, from 1964, the need to confront the possibilities for change represented by a majority Labour government. A *Private Eye* cover of that year with the Queen reading the Speech opening Parliament had her saying '. . . and I hope you realise I didn't write this crap'.

There was the possibility of an 'ultra' reaction, with consideration of a military coup linked to Lord Louis Mountbatten, but the Queen would have nothing of such plans. Instead, she adapted and with Harold Wilson, Labour Prime Minister in 1964–70 and 1974–6, developed not only a good working relationship, but also a degree of mutual affection. This was satirised in the 12 November 1965 *Private Eye* cover of Wilson formally greeting the Queen at Victoria Station after a state visit to France, with the Queen saying 'Harold, we can't go on meeting like this.'

Her relations with Edward Heath and Margaret Thatcher, Conservative Prime Ministers in 1970–4 and 1979–90 respectively, were not so close. In particular, the Queen disapproved of Thatcher's hostile stance toward the Commonwealth over its support for economic sanctions toward the apartheid regime in South Africa and was furious that she was not told in advance of the American invasion in 1983 of Grenada, a Commonwealth member. Nevertheless, the Queen attended Thatcher's funeral, a marked sign of respect.

The mood of the times, combined with advice from Wilson, encouraged attempts to make the royal family more accessible.

The *Royal Family* documentary of 1969 exposed monarchy to the close domestic scrutiny of television. Indeed, thanks to television, the royals almost became members of viewers' extended families, treated with the fascination commonly devoted to the stars of soap opera. The investiture of Charles, Prince of Wales, in 1969, a measure taken in part to assuage Welsh expectations, was also part of the televised world. In turn, *The Crown*, a later television drama series, was treated as if truthful.

With time, the Queen became an experienced and skilful adviser of successive Prime Ministers. She had political opinions, not least a belief in the Commonwealth, but was careful not to take a public political stand, and to maintain constitutional conventions. In turn, politicians helped to preserve the monarchy's neutrality. This was far from easy in the 1970s as the country moved toward chaos, not least in 1974 when the first election, held in February, left no party with a majority. Wilson was able to form a minority government, and then sought a second election to turn this into a majority. The Queen apparently insisted that this be delayed until October in order to lessen the sense of crisis.

Wilson won a small overall majority, but a malaise became readily apparent. The cover of *Private Eye* on 10 January 1975 captured this: 'Britain Sold Shock. New Man at Palace', alongside a picture of the Queen and oil-rich King Faisal of Saudi Arabia on a state visit. Faisal was more prominent in the photograph and saying 'My Wives and I'. Eighty-nine MPs voted against an increase in funding for the monarchy in 1975, while Willie Hamilton waged a long republican campaign in Parliament. As a very different instance of discontent, Marcus Serjeant, in 1981, fired six blank cartridges at the Queen as she rode down the Mall for the Trooping of the Colour royal salute, but she was unharmed and, showing considerable and characteristic presence of mind, able to calm her startled horse, Burmese.

There was a consolidation of a type, however, from 1979, with referenda in Scotland and Wales leading to the maintenance of

---

Royal Garden Party

'The Queen slowly made her way along, preceded by a posse of buffers in slightly better-fitting morning dress than the majority of the guests, and made conversation with certain selected invitees – the statutory person in a wheel chair with bearded mentor etc. When you see the Queen in the flesh she is always smaller and more beautifully made up than one remembers.'

16 July 1981, Alan Clark, *Diary*

---

constitutional arrangements. Moreover, the election of Margaret Thatcher as Prime Minister in 1979, and her re-elections in 1983 and 1987, did not appear to be a change for radicalism. She was interested in reforming British governance, but did not extend this to changing the nature of monarchy. Thatcher's innate conservatism was on display in this attitude, and the Queen rather than Thatcher was somewhat irritated by the nature of their working relationship.

Helped by the Queen's circumspect character, the royal family were able to maintain a public focus on its non-political roles, notably its importance to a host of good causes, especially voluntary organisations, at community and national level. This contributed to a strong sense that the royal family had an important purpose, and helped maintain social harmony. The emphasis on service was linked not only to charitable roles, but also to the military, and much royal time was accordingly spent on ceremonial functions.

In the 1980s and 1990s, nevertheless, the royal family, like other national institutions, was affected by the increased public criticism linked to a decline in deference. The need to consider how best to respond, both to the criticism and to the pressures of, and for, change, was further posed and accentuated by the position of the Queen's four children, which raised questions about the nature of their upbringing. The role and matrimonial difficulties of the heir, Prince Charles, proved a particularly sensitive issue. His marriage in 1981 to Lady Diana Spencer in St Paul's Cathedral had been watched on television by much of the population, and their subsequent very public rift excited a lot of attention and discussion. It culminated in divorce in 1996, Diana dramatically complaining, in a 1995 interview in *Panorama*, about Charles's continued favour for his former girlfriend, Camilla, whom he was subsequently to marry.

Although republicanism had always been at the margins in Britain from the 1790s, the 1990s saw an upsurge in anti-monarchical sentiment and a more critical press. The tragic death of Diana in August 1997 in a car accident in Paris unleashed a wave of national grief which the royal family seemed totally unable to comprehend or to respond to. At the same time, analyses of those grieving were instructive of a social politics that cohered to the issue, and, more generally, to the reputation of Princess Diana. Sadness was publicly expressed most clearly by women, the young, and homosexual men; and less so by heterosexual men, the elderly and Scots. The royal practice of 'never explain, never complain', of discretion and never expressing a personal opinion, left the Queen in a particularly difficult position in this case; although, in truth, any comments would have been risky. Moreover, she appears to be instinctively conciliatory and keen to avoid disagreements.

The new Labour government, that of Tony Blair elected in 1997, sought to encourage the monarchy to 'modernise', which, in the terms of 'New Labour', was an aspect of a discarding of the past. Royal visits became more informal, and there was a conscious effort to link royalty with the younger generation. Also in 1997, the new government proposed completely to remove the right of hereditary peers to vote in the Lords. In the event, a portion of the hereditary peerage, elected by their peers, was able

---

The Death of the Princess of Wales

'People are angry with the royal family. Blair is trying to cash in on it and the Queen has had to agree that a flag will fly at half-mast over the Palace, which has never happened before.'

4 September 1997

'. . . we've got a new monarch – Tony Blair.'

3 October 1997

Tony Benn, *Diaries*

---

to retain voting rights; but the change to the context for monarchy represented by the House of Lords, a longstanding background, was abrupt. For example, in the part of Parliament that is for the House of Lords, the iconography is very monarchical with statues and portraits of monarchs aplenty, rather than from parliamentary history. Moreover, there are rooms largely for royal purposes. At the same time, the monarchy faced no comparable constitutional change.

Neither the Blair nor the Brown governments saw any more significant developments, but the different stance of monarchy was readily apparent in 2010 when an election led to no majority. The Crown was kept informed of the coalition negotiations between Labour, the Conservatives and the Liberal Democrats, but did not play a role in a process controlled by the politicians. The monarchy validated the outcome, rather than determining, or even influencing it.

So also with successive decisions to hold referenda. Indeed, David Cameron, Conservative Prime Minister from 2010 to 2016, was criticised for revealing the Queen's pleasure when the 2014 Scottish referendum saw a clear majority of Scots who voted decide to reject independence. This represented her support for the maintenance of the United Kingdom, and her essential conservatism. Earlier, she had urged voters to think with care which was a way to urge them not to vote for independence. The attitude of the Crown to the Brexit referendum, and to the subsequent bitter constitutional impasse and political division that lasted until a general election in December 2019 delivered a verdict, was more successfully kept private. This was also the case with her view on Boris Johnson as Prime Minister. The Queen continued to hold a weekly meeting with the Prime Minister and to read daily red boxes of Cabinet papers.

Meanwhile, the issue of the succession was increasingly coming to the fore, a situation highlighted by her refusal to abdicate (unlike the example of the Dutch monarchy) and to allow the grounding of a new reign before it aged. Moreover, the length of the reign ensured that the Queen was still on the throne when rows over her son Andrew and grandson Harry came to the fore. In contrast, Pope Benedict XVI provided the example of a papal resignation in 2013, the first to do so on his own initiative since Celestine V in 1294 (Gregory XII did so in 1415 to end a schism). Nor was there need for a regency, although the 1947 Regency Act established a system of Counsellors of State to act when the monarch was abroad or ill.

Great affection and admiration for the Queen could not end discussion about the future, a situation encouraged in 2021 when the death of Prince Philip highlighted public sympathy, but also awareness of her age and frailty. In 2022, there was an increasing withdrawal from public duties, although the Queen opened the new Elizabeth underground line in London. Parliament was opened by the seventy-three-year-old Prince Charles sitting on the consort's throne; and, facing 'episodic mobility problems', which had become increasingly serious, the Queen did not attend the garden parties celebrating the Platinum Jubilee, which, instead, were hosted by other members of the royal family. Nor did she take the royal Salute at the Trooping the Colour in 2022, marking the start of national celebrations for her Platinum Jubilee, although as an instructive underlining of her preferences she was given a tour of the Chelsea Flower Show in a buggy that belongs to the royal household. The Queen took a lively interest, speaking to designers and plant experts, showing her knowledge of clematis. Yet, her withdrawal from public duties appeared increasingly apparent prior to her death on 8 September 2022, two days after a clearly frail monarch had appointed Liz Truss as Prime Minister.

Reflections on the Coronation

'While dynasties have fallen all around us, the British Throne stands more securely than ever before. If there had been any doubt it would have been dispelled by the enthusiastic multitudes who had waited in the streets for hours . . . But the most important change that has taken place with the centuries . . . is the recognition by successive rulers . . . that to reign means to serve.'

Daily Telegraph, 3 June 1953

8

Into the Future

....

Whether the British monarchy would survive became an issue of greater prominence in the early 2020s. The background had been laid in the 1960s when there was a significant breach in the continuity of both society and political culture. In 1962, for example, Sunday newspaper colour supplements began, with the first of these being the *Sunday Times*. Entitled 'A Sharp Look at the Mood of Britain', this depicted a new sense of national purpose and classlessness. A decline of formality in all respects was increasingly apparent, while the visual identifiers of class, position and status were mocked and abandoned and became less common. A set of values and practices that had provided cohesion and continuity, at least since the mid-nineteenth century, and often for far longer, was much challenged or, in part, collapsed. Respect for the monarchy, the Church of England, Parliament, the legal system, the military, the nation's past, unwavering support for the union with Scotland, for the landed Protestant ascendancy in Northern Ireland and for much else, including the rural railways destroyed after the Beeching Report, were all eroded. This erosion occurred in response to a widespread mood for change expressed in terms of shifts in the understanding of gender, youth, class, place, nation and race.

At the same time, the monarchy was no simple passive counter. For example, a major part of the Queen's effort was the idea that the Commonwealth could be a lasting and successful sequel to the Empire, with its nations all equal. There was some success for the Commonwealth for a while, not only in Britain where I can remember several visits as a child to the Commonwealth Institute, but also across much of the former empire as a new international identity was defined. Indeed the Commonwealth became a way to maintain links and to align the Non-Aligned World with the West in the shape of Britain.

However, it proved difficult to sustain this achievement. Few Britons, beside Elizabeth II, took much interest in the Commonwealth from the late 1980s; and, as a force for identity, it succumbed to the reality of different concerns and roles. These included Britain's trans-Atlantic links and its European role as a member of the European Economic Community, later European Union, from 1973 to 2019. The closing of the Commonwealth Institute in London was more widely symptomatic. Originally the Imperial Institute, established by royal charter in 1887, its name was changed to the Commonwealth Institute in 1958, but, following its sale in 2007, it became, in 2016, the home of the Design Museum. Similarly, after a very brief and unsuccessful history, the newly established British Empire and Commonwealth Museum in Bristol closed in 2009.

Such an account provides a bleak background for the continuation of monarchy, making it appear an aspect of the past that has somehow dodged the bullet of time, but only so far. This process can then be explained in terms of conservatism, the 'false consciousness' of much of the public, and, separately, the personal popularity of the Queen. Yet, from this perspective, the writing is on the wall for monarchy, to employ one of the frequently rolled-out phrases. There is discussion as to whether King Charles III, whom the Queen before her death ensured would already be head of the Commonwealth, will be the last monarch, and public speculation in modern times about the future of the monarchy has never been so sustained.

Two caveats can at once be offered. First, commentators have earlier noted considerable change that made much or all of the *ancien régime* appear dated, if not redundant. Democracy, industrialisation, large-scale urbanisation and modernism can all be considered in that light. The relevance of George V to the 1920s of electricity and the motorcar can also be questioned. And yet, monarchy had translated well to the practicalities of the possible, as with George V's radio broadcasts, appearance at football matches, and visits to people's homes. Moreover, far from democracy, as measured by the extensions to the franchise in 1918 and 1928 to include all men and women aged twenty-one or above, leading to republicanism or Communism, instead Conservative or Conservative-dominated ministries held power for most of the period 1918–2022, while Labour ministries were scarcely radical, let alone republican.

Secondly, monarchy could move to the modern. This was seen by a host of gestures and moments during Elizabeth II's reign. They took very varied form as befitted her activities and responsibilities. Thus, in 1987, she amended the statutes of the most distinguished of British chivalric orders, the Order of the Garter, to permit the admission of women on terms equal to those of the Knights Companion of the Order. Alternatively, in 2002, the celebration of her Golden Jubilee brought carnival dancers and gospel singers into the Mall. The royal walkabout began, in Coventry, in 1970, and from 1993 parts of Buckingham Palace were opened to tourists. The Jubilee tours from 1977 revealed great popularity. In 2001, the Queen visited the *EastEnders* set, while Prince Charles featured in an episode of *Coronation Street* in 2000 and of *EastEnders* in 2022. The 2012 Diamond Jubilee was folded in with the London Olympics, but there were 9,500 road closures to permit street parties.

For the Platinum Jubilee in 2022, the Local Government Association predicted more than 16,000 approved street parties, including 475 in Hertfordshire; but about fifteen million people taking part in neighbourhood events, including eight million in street parties. The Jubilee saw a number of activities close to the Crown, from a 124-gun salute from the Tower of London and a service of thanksgiving for the Queen's reign at St Paul's Cathedral, to the Epsom Derby (horse-racing).

The entire occasion served as a reminder of the role of the monarchy in collective identity. It offered an opportunity for the British to consider who they were supposed to be and what they once were, and also was a major factor in tourism. Without monarchy, there was not the pomp and circumstance joining all these elements.

In the European case, monarchy has been shown to be compatible with the idea of the irresistibility of the democratic impulse. The 'reign not rule' model is to the fore, with seemingly little fear of a Putinesque figure emerging. It is apparently safer that way with a hereditary system than with a superficially elective one.

The survival of monarchy then is a classic instance of the nature of history. It invites discussion in terms of the fundamental contrast between interpretations that see change as arising due to crisis and those that emphasise adaptability. The latter is very much part of the self-image of the monarchy and, indeed, an aspect of an understanding of monarchy, by a society that is inherently changing, not least due to its embrace of multicultural ideology and practice. Monarchy has to adapt to this. Alternatively, the emphasis on crisis would focus on the culture wars of the early twenty-first century and argue that the contention and controversies involved make such adaptability more difficult, if not impossible.

The response to imminent change at the top in the early 2020s played through this issue. There are questions around how Charles III would be able to match the difficulties posed by his mother's legacy of quiet service and, separately, public expectations about the monarchy now and in the future. In particular, the directness of Charles as Prince of Wales, and his strong commitment to environmental issues, may be less easy to accept and manage now he is king, not least as it serves as a major contrast to Elizabeth II's circumspection. In 2022, he caused controversy with his views on the expulsion of illegal immigrants.

The constitutional relationship between Crown and Parliament requires a sense of tradition, decorum and practical politics.

Conversely, Charles's environmental concerns may make him appear particularly relevant, and also his commitment to being a 'monarch of all faiths'. There are choices to be made, and these also reflect a theme frequently seen, of how the personalities of monarchs make them effective or ineffective rulers and contribute to the evolution of the monarchy. The Prince's Trust has played a very major role in philanthropy, just as the Duke of Edinburgh Scheme remains crucial to a broad concept of education. Other major commitments included that of the highly effective Princess Anne to the Save the Children Fund.

In his *Telegraph* interview of June 2022, Gordon Brown, a former Prime Minister, remarked:

> My advice to the monarchy . . . is not to be seen all the time in aristocratic settings, but to meet people where they are in all the different communities of the country. And the danger for any privileged group of people who have got status and power in this country, is that they're remote from the people they represent.

Responses to a number of lesser issues have played separate roles in making the monarchy appear to be having difficulties in matching public moods. This includes the questioning of Prince Andrew's personal life, notably his serious lack of judgment over his friendship with Jeffrey Epstein, and, very differently, the controversy that has surrounded the alleged royal response to the Duke and Duchess of Sussex, Harry and Meghan. The latter came more to the fore as the issue appeared to undercut suggestions of modernity and openness to multiculturalism. In practice, there has been a greater degree of scepticism in Britain than in America about the Sussexes; as with a critical Hilary Rose in *The Times* on 19 May 2022 imagining the Duchess telling Netflix: 'we have to keep slagging off the entire royal family to keep ourselves in the public eye ... Our goal was always to make a modern royal family.' The resentments manifested by the Sussexes have been portrayed by most of the British press as narcissistic and self-important.

The Duke and Duchess of Cambridge (William and Kate) have so far had a far less bumpy ride from the media because they are generally regarded as selfless and conscientious. Their tour to the West Indies in 2022 was treated as a failure, due to looking dated, as with taking the salute from an open Land Rover; but the scale of the opposition they encountered was exaggerated. Moreover, it is natural that independent countries there should envisage a republican future. In a 1999 referendum, Australia rejected by about 55 to 45 per cent removing the Queen as head of state; but a new republican government under an open republican was elected in 2022.

Birth of Elizabeth II

'I have a feeling the child will be Queen of England and perhaps the last sovereign.'

Diary of 'Chips' Channon, 21 April 1926

There were three main questions in 2022 about the British monarchy. First, would it survive; second, in what form; and, third, what role would it have outside Britain? There was also the question of how far Britain, let alone the United Kingdom, could continue to operate. In particular, the prospect of Scotland, once independent, maintaining monarchical links was increasingly problematic. So, even more, with the future of monarchy in Northern Ireland, as the possibility of the reunification of Ireland gathered pace there following elections in Northern Ireland in 2022.

As a 'dignified', let alone an 'efficient', part of the constitution, monarchy appeared redundant to many. That a sense of foreboding rather than opportunity is to the fore is not so much a comment on King Charles III, who has earned more respect in recent years, as a product of the profound respect and deep affection felt for Queen Elizabeth. The latter poses a formidable challenge to Charles. Yet the reign of Edward VII in the aftermath of the long period when Victoria had been on the throne, shows that it is still possible to make a significant contribution in this context.

Those who thought monarchy redundant remained a clear minority, however; one that was enhanced by the difficulty of agreeing on any specific replacement. Indeed, in some respects, a presidency would represent the continuation of monarchy in another form. Moreover, the history of monarchy suggested an ability to regenerate the institution and practice that holds out hope for the future; and for the monarchy as well as Britain.

The Saxon Kings of the English

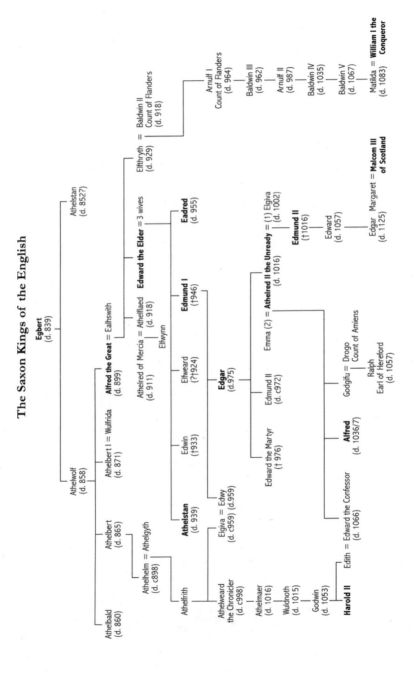

The House of Normandy

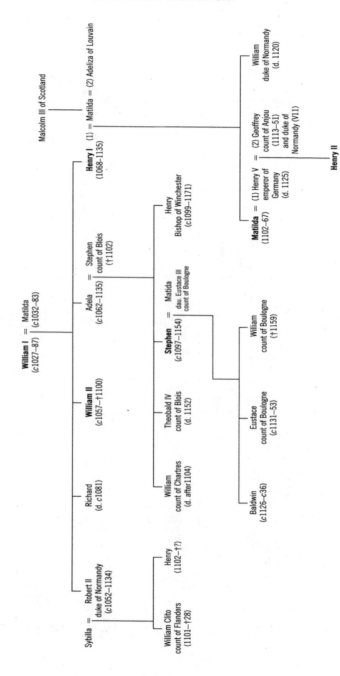

228

The House of Anjou/ Plantagenet

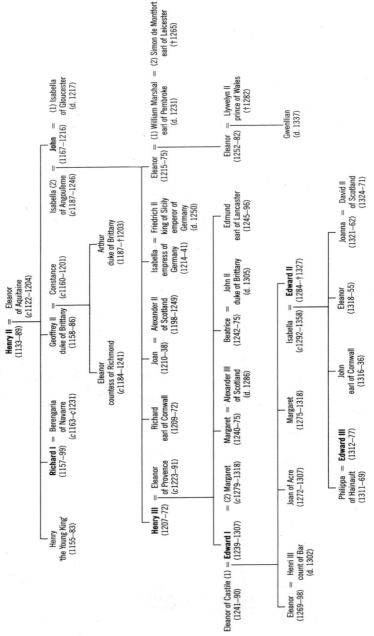

The Houses of York and Lancaster

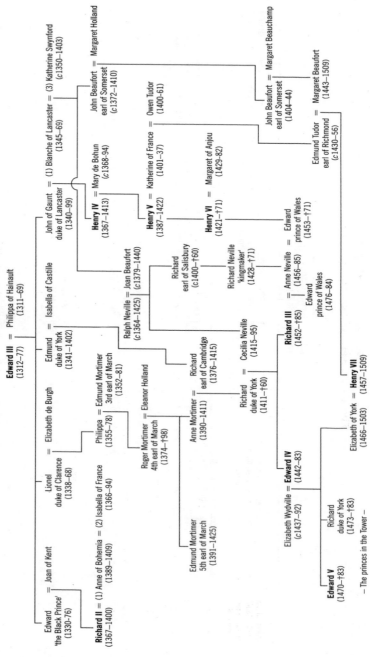

The Tudor and Stewart Succession

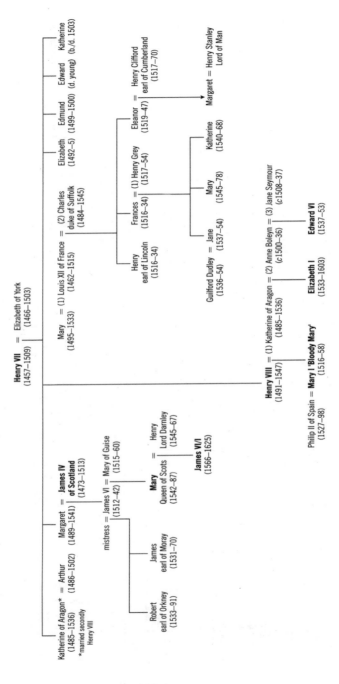

Henry VII (1457–1509) = Elizabeth of York (1466–1503)

Katherine of Aragon* (1485–1536) = Arthur (1486–1502)
*married secondly Henry VIII

Margaret (1489–1541) = James IV of Scotland (1473–1513)

mistress = James V (1512–42) = Mary of Guise (1515–60)

Robert earl of Orkney (1533–91)

James earl of Moray (1531–70)

Mary Queen of Scots (1542–87) = Henry Lord Darnley (1545–67)

James VI/I (1566–1625)

Mary (1495–1533) = (1) Louis XII of France (1462–1515) = (2) Charles duke of Suffolk (1484–1545)

Henry earl of Lincoln (1516–34)

Frances (1516–34) = (1) Henry Grey (1517–54)

Eleanor (1519–47) = Henry Clifford earl of Cumberland (1517–70)

Margaret = Henry Stanley Lord of Man

Guilford Dudley (1536–54) = Jane (1537–54)

Mary (1545–78)

Katherine (1540–68)

Elizabeth (1492–5)

Edmund (1499–1500)

Edward (d. young)

Katherine (b./d. 1503)

Henry VIII (1491–1547) = (1) Katherine of Aragon (1485–1536) = (2) Anne Boleyn (1500–36) = (3) Jane Seymour (c1508–37)

Philip II of Spain (1527–98) = Mary I 'Bloody Mary' (1516–58)

Elizabeth I (1533–1603)

Edward VI (1537–53)

231

The House of Stewart

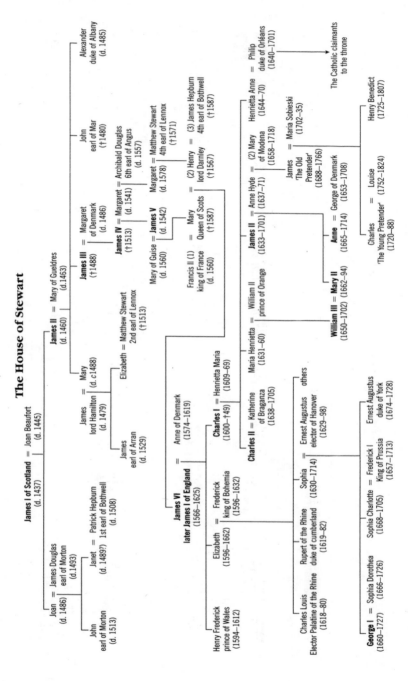

The House of Hanover

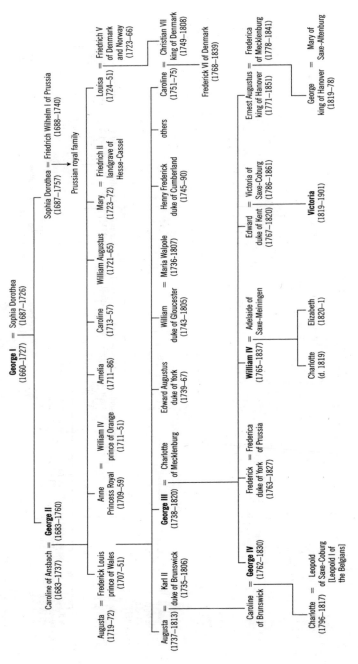

The Houses of Saxe-Coburg-Gotha (changed to Windsor)

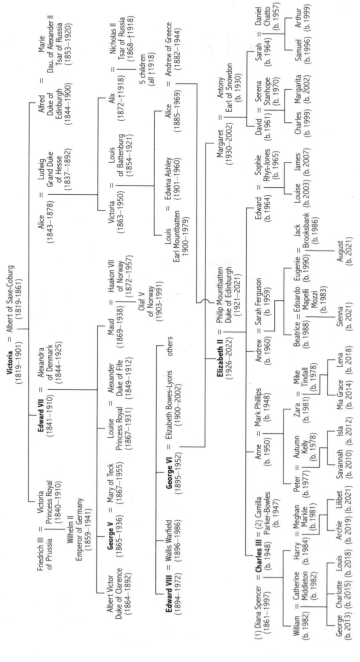

Selected Further Reading

....

The two major series of monarchical biographies are published by Yale and Penguin. The former are more substantial and scholarly, the latter shorter and, to a degree, more impressionistic. As with any series, some are more successful than others, but all deserve attention. In general, the more recent can be better, as they can draw on more scholarship, but there are significant exceptions. Moreover, in certain cases, there are weaknesses with the volumes in both series. The following is a list, by no means exhaustive, of the better volumes, by monarch in chronological order, rather than by author.

For individual monarchs, the following are particularly recommended:

Athelstan	Foot, Sarah
Aethelred the Unready	Abels, Richard
Cnut	Lavelle, Ryan
Edward the Confessor	Barlow, Frank
William I	Douglas, David
William II	Barlow, Frank
Henry I	Hollister, C. Warren
Stephen	Watkins, Carl
Henry II	Warren, W. L.
Richard I	Gillingham, John
John	Warner, W. L.
Henry III	Carpenter, David
Edward I	King, Andy and Andrew Spencer (eds), *Edward I: New Interpretations* (2020)
Edward II	Maddcott, John

Edward III	Sumption, John
Richard II	Saul, Nigel
Henry IV	Nall, Catherine
Henry V	Allmand, Christopher
Henry VI	Wolffe, Bertram
Edward IV	Ross, Charles
Edward V	Penn, Thomas
Richard III	Ross, Charles
Henry VII	Cunningham, Sean
Henry VIII	Scarisbrick, John
Edward VI	Alford, Stephen
Mary I	Edwards, John
Elizabeth I	Castor, Helen
James I	Cogswell, Thomas
Charles I	Kishlansky, Mark
Charles II	Jackson, Clare
James II	Miller, John
William III and Mary II	Keates, Jonathan
Anne	Gregg, Edward
George I	Hatton, Ragnhild
George II	Black, Jeremy
George III	Black, Jeremy
George IV	Smith, E. A.
William IV	Knight, Roger
Victoria	Ridley, Jane
Edward VII	Davenport-Hines, Richard
George V	Cannadine, David
Edward VIII	Brendon, Piers
George VI	Ziegler, Philip
Elizabeth II	Hurd, Douglas

In addition, it is worth reading:
Bates, David, Julia Crick and Sarah Hamilton (eds), *Writing Medieval Biography 750–1250* (2006)

SELECTED FURTHER READING

Bogdanor, Vernon, *The Monarchy and the Constitution* (1995)
Cannon, John and Ralph Griffiths (eds), *The Oxford Illustrated History of the British Monarchy* (1988)

Index